ENVIRONOMICS

Environomics

THE ECONOMICS OF ENVIRONMENTALLY SAFE PROSPERITY

Farid A. Khavari

Westport, Connecticut
London

Library of Congress Cataloging-in-Publication Data

Khavari, Farid A.
  Environomics : the economics of environmentally safe prosperity /
Farid A. Khavari.
      p.   cm.
  Includes bibliographical references and index.
  ISBN 0-275-94462-X (alk. paper)
  1. Economic development—Environmental aspects. 2. Sustainable
development. I. Title.
  HD75.6.K485 1993
  363.7'07—dc20   92-37527

British Library Cataloguing in Publication Data is available.

Library of Congress Catalog Card Number: 92-37527
ISBN: 0-275-94462-X

First published in 1993

Praeger Publishers, 88 Post Road West, Westport, CT 06881
An imprint of Greenwood Publishing Group, Inc.

Printed in the United States of America

The paper used in this book complies with the
Permanent Paper Standard issued by the National
Information Standards Organization (Z39.48–1984).

10   9   8   7   6   5   4   3   2   1

For my loving wife, Janilla,
and our wonderful children,
Armin and Bianca.

I hope that this book will help
to make the world a better place
for them and for generations to come.

Contents

Preface

The vision presented in this work is grounded in the global economic and ecological realities that determine the social structures of our lives. How we deal with these issues will shape the legacy we leave to our children. How we reconcile a vibrant economic life and sustainable environment will dictate, to a great extent, how future generations will live.

So far, humanity has survived a variety of social disasters, but humanity is currently at an unprecedented historical juncture. We are now creating an environment so putrid and a social structure so bankrupt that future generations will regard us with disdain and find it impossible to forgive us for what we have done. If we continue unabatedly in this direction, history will call our era a dark age.

Economic growth in the conventional sense does not contribute to real economic growth in any abiding manner. Growth as we have sought and achieved it is rapidly exhausting the earth's limited raw materials, materials that will be needed even more urgently by those who come after us. History will show that the pollution generated by our current way of life began the ultimate destruction of habitable areas. If such a legacy is to be avoided, we must begin now to change the equation between economic growth and environmental destruction.

This work explores the manner in which a general prosperity may be attained while overall environmental conditions are improved (or, at least, not further threatened). It is my hope that this work can show a way to benefit the human spirit, to avoid a mass catastrophe of our making, and, perhaps, to rewrite history before it happens.

1

Introduction

The tragedy of our time is that, although humanity's pursuit of economic interests inflicts irreparable devastation on the planet, long-term economic progress is not achieved. For the most part, environmental problems are the result of economic activity and are economic problems. Environmental problems can be solved only if economic activity is channeled in ways that are environmentally safe. Otherwise, any attempt to resolve environmental problems is futile.

People are not inclined to make economic sacrifices for environmental improvement, whether that sacrifice involves the reduction of a prosperous standard of living or a struggle for mere survival. Few citizens of the industrialized nations would be willing to give up their automobiles, although they may be well aware that their cars pollute the environment. Brazilian peasants are even less likely to forego their destruction of rain forests, regardless of the global impact of such activities, when the alternative is starvation. It is impractical to expect people who are uncertain of their supper to be concerned about future generations, just as it is naive to expect people who could afford to do so to act on such if it would cause inconvenience.

Clearly, any solution leading to the preservation of the environment must address economic needs. Just as we would not sacrifice the earth in the name of quality of life, we should not sacrifice quality of life, or life itself, to preserve the earth.

Environmental issues are global, not local. The use of an aerosol can of hair spray or deodorant in Des Moines, Iowa, nibbles at the ozone layer and can contribute to a drought in Bangladesh; destruction of a rain forest in South America impacts the climate and atmosphere of countries in Eastern Europe. Any solution to environmental problems must be global in scope and therefore must address the economic needs of everyone on earth. Rain forests cannot be saved unless the people currently reliant on those resources can be independent of them. The pollution caused by automobiles cannot be eliminated unless alternative transportation exists or nonpolluting vehicles are developed.

Until now, these issues have made adversaries of economists and environmentalists. Progress has been slow and fitful as the idealism of the environmentalists confronts the power of economic interests, seemingly at every turn. Never mind prosperity or comfort, the environmentalists seem to say, if that new power plant or that logging operation threatens some obscure species. To hell with snail darters and owls, the economists seem to respond, give us jobs and growth!

Unfortunately, uncontrolled economic growth has caused lasting damage to the earth without creating prosperity. However, the solutions proposed by the environmentalists usually lack attention to economic needs and thus are equally impractical in any long-range sense.

There will be no solution to environmental problems until both sides recognize that environmental problems are economic problems, and vice versa. As yet, neither the economists nor the environmentalists have acknowledged the indivisible relationship of environmental and economic problems or their global nature. In general, the environmentalists tend to focus on relatively narrow issues, such as protection of a particular species, a rain forest in southern Brazil, or the wet lands in Alaska or the banning of nuclear power, without regard for the economic impact of the realization of their goals. Economists, on the other hand, tend to dismiss the environmental impact of an industry or a project as a necessary cost of doing business. Economic growth creates prosperity, the economists reason, and if pollution is a by-product of economic worth, then we will create further growth by cleaning up the mess. If a natural resource is depleted, a strong economy simply will come up with a substitute for it. The economists seem to believe that growth per se is a worthy goal and that there are no inherent limits to it.

To date, "growth," in the conventional sense, has meant a quantitative increase in the production of goods. This is, in fact, counterproductive, because it destroys the environment and exhausts our natural resources but does not create lasting prosperity in any real sense.

The obsessive obstinacy of the environmentalists is equally counterproductive. By ignoring economic needs, the environmentalists disregard simple human nature. If a person is freezing, he will burn his house to get warm if there is nothing else to burn; what good is his house, if he has frozen to death? If a person is starving, he will eat the seeds saved for next year's crop; what good is next year's crop if he has starved to death while waiting? Before people can be concerned about the future of the planet, they must have assurance of their personal survival in the present. The key to the coexistence of people and their environment is economic measures that assure the survival of both.

As long as the relationship between the environmentalists and the economists is adversarial, there will be no solution. There is no question that serious efforts must be made to preserve the environment, and there is no doubt that this can be achieved only in a climate of general prosperity. If economic growth is necessary to foster environmental improvements but at the same time is inimical to the interests of the environment, what can we do?

A first step is to understand that the relationship between the environment and the economy is not a two-sided issue. Political, social, religious, and technological factors play substantial roles and cannot be ignored. These factors can either help to alleviate or act to exacerbate the situation.

Many people suggest simple solutions. For example, some believe that if all the nations of the world would redirect a tiny fraction of their military budgets toward the economic well-being of their people, many of the world's economic problems could be resolved and poverty could be eliminated. In addition, such measures would prevent the environmental destruction resulting from war. There is little doubt that a redistribution of resources along these lines would improve matters and perhaps prevent ecoterrorism of the sort epitomized by the burning of Kuwait in 1991, but such simplistic notions ignore the fact that the diversion of funds from production of weapons to that of consumer goods and services would not alter the balance between economics as we know it and the destruction of the environment. Despite short-term improvements in standards of living and some economic gains, little lasting prosperity would be created.

Other laudable but inadequate suggestions include recycling waste materials into new products and increasing the utilization of benign and environmentally safe technologies combined with the development of renewable energy resources, such as solar, wind, and geothermal approaches. Certainly these are steps in the right direction, but they are too little, incomplete, and insignificant to provide a comprehensive solution to both the economic and environmental problems.

We realize that legislation is necessary to protect endangered species, forests, and air and water resources and to prohibit the use of certain materials, products, and technologies that are environmentally destructive. This legislation, however, is usually localized and does not help solve the worldwide problems. In the long run, all efforts to preserve the environment can succeed only if they are coupled to a new approach to economics.

The purpose of this book is to demonstrate how the environment can be preserved in a new era of environmentally safe general prosperity. The new economic concepts presented here are adaptable to both the industrial and the service sectors of the economy. The word "environomics" has been coined to represent the economic concept introduced here — environmentally safe prosperity. New definitions and explanations are included, defining concepts that are neglected by conventional economic theories.

This book is not another compendium of our environmental troubles or a catalog of individual solutions. Its perspective is aerial, macroscopic. It is hoped that from this vantage point, the reader will see all our environmental problems as interrelated and inextricably dependent upon economic remedies for their permanent solution.

The era of economics as we have known it is over. We have exploited our natural resources and damaged the environment, but we have not achieved real prosperity in any enduring sense. Now is the time for a new economics committed to true and lasting general prosperity in a safe, clean environment: environomics.

2

Environomics Explored

Environomics is a practical approach to resolving the world's environmental problems while revitalizing and redirecting economic activities to create permanent prosperity for humanity. The application of the concepts presented here will result in both the preservation and the repair of the environment and in the establishment of a higher standard of living for everyone sharing our planet.

A utopian vision? Perhaps. Perhaps, one even surpassing previous utopian ideals. To most individuals it is almost unbelievable that the eternal conflict between economic growth and a healthy environment can be resolved. Even more amazing is the potential that this new socioeconomic vision could foster general prosperity with a balanced ecology.

Until now, the necessity of a trade-off between economic prosperity and ecology has been taken for granted. It has always been assumed that greater prosperity meant deterioration of the environment; conversely, maintaining a healthy environment meant settling for a lower standard of living. Environomics shows that these assumptions are unwarranted. The world can be an integrated whole, at peace with itself, largely because prosperity has been fairly distributed within a safe environment.

Nations employing the concepts of environomics would no longer need to exploit other nations. The planet would no longer need to be plundered and destroyed in the interest of survival. Daily life would no longer need to be fraught with almost constant worry over financial obligations. The anxiety over earning money for food, clothing, shelter, health care, education, and transportation could be removed. Unemployment, homelessness, starvation, and other extremes of human degradation could be eliminated. Environomics will change our philosophy of allocation, production, and distribution of available resources, and every person will have access to all basic necessities.

The possibility of owning a home will be a reality for everyone, rather than only a dream for most, and it will not take complicated measures to purchase it or a lifetime to pay for it. People will realize the benefits of universal access to quality health care and education at affordable costs. Social security for everyone will be a fact of life, while everyone contributes to funding it at a modest rate.

Our vocabulary will change, too. Words like "recession," "inflation," "stagflation," "unemployment," "trade balance deficit," "budget deficit," and the like will be archaic. Concepts such as "sluggish economic growth" and "raiding Social Security funds" will be obsolete under environomics.

It is hard to believe that this economic vision and its concepts were not anticipated and integrated into the great economic engines of socialism or capitalism. These concepts are remarkably simple and logical, providing a basis for a workable world economy.

The best news is that by following the principles of environomics, all nations and their peoples will achieve general prosperity with no further damage to the environment. This new way of life will actually act to reinvigorate the planet. Rain forests will be recovered, ozone holes filled, the threats of nuclear war and nuclear waste eliminated, populations stabilized, and global warming neutralized. Los Angeles, New York, Mexico City, Tokyo, and Detroit will have clean air again, safe to breathe. Our rivers and oceans will produce fish and seafood not contaminated with mercury or other toxins. The air and water everywhere will be clean, and plants will be healthy and vigorous. Most important, people will be much healthier. They will have time to relax and commune with nature once disease and social stresses have been substantially reduced.

New ideas are funny things. A few people can immediately grasp a new concept or a new logic, but many cannot or, perhaps, will not. It may be that people have to come to a point where they have no other choice.

The industrialized nations have plundered the globe's natural resources, polluted the ecosystem, and escalated an insane arms race, all to maintain power and to gain wealth. At the same time, the less-fortunate nations are suffering and starving, neglected. Even when a need for limits to runaway greed have become apparent, the leaders of the world have taken no definite steps to change these suicidal tendencies, unwilling to give an inch in their drive for supremacy.

Fortunately, the grim limits to conventional concepts of growth are forcing leaders to rethink their precarious and illusory sense of wealth and security. They have no choice but to give serious consideration to alternatives that have the potential to save them from themselves.

The time is right for environonomics, a concept designed to revive a dying planet and its starving economies, and to awaken an age of global prosperity, peace, and environmental harmony.

3

The Circle of Environmental Destruction and Poverty

If we are to change our current status, we need to understand how we have come to be in our current worldwide situation. It has been a gradual process, allowing us to accept practices and policies slowly without recognizing their potential dangers and ramifications.

Several years ago, a scheme called "pyramid" spread across the United States, until it was declared unlawful and was banned. A few people got together and started a profitable economic game, making themselves the top of the pyramid. Each person recruited more people into the scheme and collected money from them. The new recruits recruited others, collected money from them, and passed part of the money upward to the top of the pyramid while keeping a portion for themselves. The fresh recruits recruited more, and so on. As more and more people came into the pyramid, those closest to the top made more money, and the top position was a bonanza. The people on the bottom of the pyramid paid into the scheme but got nothing out of it until a new bottom layer was created. The excitement soon would have been over even if the authorities had not stopped it. Obviously, such a scheme required a lot of people to give up money for a few people to get a lot.

Recently, the pyramid concept has been applied in multilevel marketing programs, with much the same results. Many companies who market their products in this manner make a tremendous amount of money, a few higher-level distributors make a lot of money, a large number in the middle of the distribution process make some money, and plenty of others end up with little more than a lot of products and dreams of selling distributorships to others who would be below them on the pyramid.

Pyramiding is not a new scheme. A man named Charles Ponzi invented a process whereby investors were paid handsome returns on their investments, these dividends (or profits) being funded by fresh

investors. Like the pyramid, the Ponzi scheme could be sustained only
for so long, until he ran out of investors.

Today, we know there is no free lunch for everybody. In reality, a lot
of people bear the burden for a few to become wealthy. As long as it
seems that everyone can become wealthy, everyone is willing to play and
the base of the pyramid is maintained. The fallacy is in the belief that any
of these schemes create wealth. In fact, they simply redistribute money
from large numbers of people to small numbers of people. Wealth is not
created, but a comparatively small group of powerful and wealthy
individuals emerges.

One analogy often cited in economics is that of ripples created by
dropping a stone in the center of a pond. This is said to represent
economic growth, radiating prosperity from the center (the richest part of
the population) outward to the poorer people. A more apt comparison
would be that this represents the ripple effect of environmental problems,
which grow as prosperity decreases.

In the 1960s, in light of the economic miracles achieved in postwar
West Germany and Japan, it seemed that the solution to all problems lay
in economic growth, with no limits foreseen. Seminars concerning
various concepts of economic growth were well attended. Robert Solow,
an economic guru at the Massachusetts Institute of Technology, developed a model for economic growth that became famous as the Solow
Model. His theories excited many students of economics, and he
preached his "golden rule of economic growth" far and wide. The Solow
Model epitomized economic thoughts in the 1960s, just as it embodied
the flaw common to virtually all theories of the period, that is, the
assumption that there is no limit to potential economic growth.

Simply put, virtually all economists agree that the key to economic
growth is production. In textbook terms, production is a function of
combining capital and labor. Proponents of conventional economic
growth believe that given sufficient capital and labor, anything, in any
quantity, can be produced as desired or required.

One might well ask, what about other details, such as raw materials,
energy, technology, space, and the environment? The assumption has
always been that as long as sufficient capital and labor were present, the
rest could be made available. Perhaps, in theory, some resources might
be exhausted eventually, but there would always be substitutes. Plainly,
this thinking is flawed. What can we substitute for clean air and water,
even if we could replace crude oil somewhere down the line?

It is becoming clear that the economic growth promoted in conventional models is not sustainable in the long term. Even after a few

decades, the depletion of resources and the havoc wrought on the environment will affect the quality of life for generations to come.

The events of the 1970s and 1980s underscore the futility of the pursuit of these economic theories. It is disappointing to note that in spite of the consequences that are becoming more evident every day, economic thought and theory have changed very little.

In order to understand and realize the scope of the problems that plague us, it is necessary to go through the origins of them, not getting into details, but merely pointing out the major problems we have in the areas of ecology, economics, technology, and politics — problems that have contributed to our current negative situation. After identification of these problems and the areas from which they stem, the solutions will be explored in subsequent chapters.

The problems regarding the environment, economy, technology, and politics are so interrelated, so complex, that they must be viewed as a whole. A temporary or piecemeal solution to one problem will not provide a method of preventing future disasters. If we are to achieve comprehensive and satisfactory results, we must address all problem areas, seeking the basis of the problem and applying a solution at the root of the destruction.

The intention, therefore, is to search for global solutions and approaches, rather than for detailed answers to individual questions in each area. For example, there is no point in answering the specific needs of an individual company or industry if we have not identified the effects of their global behavior in a given economy or, for that matter, in a worldwide economy. The goal is to determine how the needs of companies and industries affect our natural resources and environment, as well as what effect they have on the population's level of prosperity.

The most pressing of all are the environmental issues. At the rate we are going, we are headed toward destruction and extinction, as previously mentioned. Much of this is the result of our current approach to economics, both the economic activities practiced by the poor people and nations, who act in the interest of survival, and the actions of rich people and nations, who act to prosper further. The economics of the world are largely dictated by politics and by the technology required to support the economic practices. Our current approach is uncontrolled and destructive throughout all of these activities.

Ecological problems are not limited to one or two issues. They are, unfortunately, multifarious. The diversity of these problems can be seen in their effects throughout the environment — on land, ocean, drinking water, animal and fish habitations, and rain forests, to name a few. The negative effects on human health, as well as on the planet, are becoming increasingly more important to the growing population of the world.

All of us were shocked by the results of the meltdown of the Chernobyl nuclear power plant in the Soviet Union. There were terrifying pictures of children with deformed faces and bodies, deformities resulting from the contamination of the area by the radioactive rays. Pictures of donkeys with six legs provided another example of the frightening effects of radioactivity. Most horrifying was the realization that this nightmare could occur anywhere in the world, wherever a nuclear power plant was in operation.

There is no lack of information regarding ecological problems — this entire book could be devoted to the documentation of the environmental issues. However, the purpose of this book is not to list the individual problems but to identify them and, in a general manner, seek a comprehensive solution.

If one had to select a single point from which to start, the economic activities of the world's populations would have to be chosen. It is frustrating, yet true, that in spite of the exploitation of natural resources, in spite of severe environmental damage in the name of economic gain, we are still unable to satisfy the primary needs of the world's population. Even in the richest countries in the world, even in the United States, there are people who do not have sufficient food, shelter, or health care. If these needs are not being met in the advanced and developed nations, imagine the problems of basic survival in the Third World countries. A very small percentage of the world's population enjoy a luxurious standard of living, engaging in destructive economic activities that cut away at the very foundation of the balance of the people. During the 1960s, the earth's population was said to be 800 million rich people and almost 2.4 billion poor; by the year 2000, this could become 800 million rich people and almost 6.5 billion poor.

The primary goal of economic activity should be to satisfy the basic needs of all people, that is, food, clothing, housing, health care, and security for people in their advanced years. Once that is accomplished — and only after that has been accomplished — a higher standard of living for everyone can be addressed, a standard that includes tangible items like cars and televisions and intangible items like vacations and cultural events. Most important, this must be achieved without putting any further burden on our natural resources or the environment. Economic activities must be directed into the proper channels and correctly executed to attain these goals. At this point in time, we are doing exactly the opposite.

There are four major areas that lead to our current destructive cycle, and these areas are interactive. Economic growth, technology, politics, and energy requirements must be addressed on an overall basis. We will consider these first on the stationary and then on the dynamic models.

Based on conventional economic concepts, if the intention is to achieve economic growth, it will lead to increased use of energy and raw materials, causing further environmental problems. To eliminate the ecological problems caused by this activity, further use of energy will be necessary for cleaning up or recycling by-products. The cost of cleaning up, documented as a "social cost," reduces the achieved economic growth and increases the burden on the ecology because of the environmentally unfriendly characteristics of the used energy sources. On the other hand, the increased energy consumption contributes to the shrinking of the existing energy reserves or requires the development of new or alternate energy reserves. Because the required high cost of investment for the development of new energy sources must be generated by increased economic growth, further employment of energy becomes necessary. The cycle begins again from the beginning, creating a vicious circle, as illustrated in Figure 3.1.

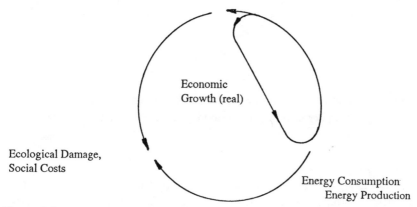

Figure 3.1
Stationary Model Demonstrating the Consequences of Using Environmentally Damaging *versus* Environmentally Friendly Energy Resources — Nominal Economic Growth

In either case, the result is increased use of energy. However, when a certain point is reached, employed energy contributes to a diminished return. Figures 3.1 and 3.2 show the need for the following considerations in energy use.

1. Economic growth is worth the effort only when it does not take place at the expense of the environment.
2. In order to prevent damage to the ecology, it is necessary to develop environmentally friendly, alternate energy resources.
3. To make the high cost of investment profitable, use of inexhaustible energy resources must be enforced while the alternate sources are being developed.

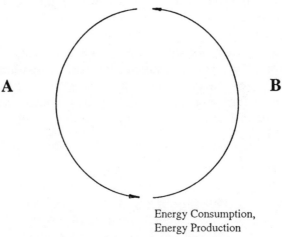

A   B

Energy Consumption,
Energy Production

Figure 3.2
Stationary Model Demonstrating the Consequences of Using Environmentally Damaging *versus* Environmentally Friendly Energy Resources — Real Economic Growth

If humanity would develop only environmentally friendly and inexhaustible alternate energy sources and use them exclusively, the immediate adverse effects on the ecology would be eliminated, resulting in elimination of the social cost. Implementation of this concept would lead to the results depicted in Figure 3.2, in which energy usage contributes to economic growth. Part of that achieved economic growth must be reinvested to cover the expenses caused by adaptation or conversion of technological progress or maintenance of the energy plants. However, the half circle "A" becomes smaller and smaller as time passes, without ever disappearing. On the other hand, the half circle "B" expands itself permanently, as Figure 3.3 illustrates.

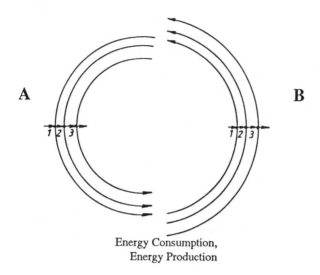

Energy Consumption,
Energy Production

Figure 3.3
The Use of Environmentally Damaging and Exhaustible *versus*
Environmentally Friendly and Inexhaustible Energy Resources in
Evolutionary (Dynamic) Models — Real Economic Growth

Given these considerations, one comes to the conclusion that with the use of each unit of energy, the achieved economic growth would expand in real terms. In other words, to achieve the same economic growth, less energy would be needed. With increased use of energy, the economic growth would be progressive. Conversely, the use of environmentally damaging and exhaustive energy resources would likely result in the circle shown in Figure 3.4. More energy would be required to achieve economic growth, as well as to clean up the resultant ecological damages. In this instance, the achieved economic growth decreases in real terms because of the social costs and the required investment for producing yet more energy.

If this issue is not realized and dealt with effectively, the environmental damage and social costs could become infinite. Most likely, the combination of these two, increasing indefinitely, would complete the circle of environmental destruction and poverty.

To better understand our present situation, let us explore some of the misconceptions of our current economic theories and practices.

One of the improper economic activities currently practiced is the production of low-quality products with a short life span. The effects of

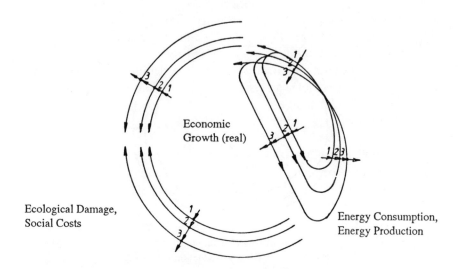

Figure 3.4
The Use of Environmentally Damaging and Exhaustible *versus*
Environmentally Friendly and Inexhaustible Energy Resources in
Evolutionary (Dynamic) Models — Nominal Economic Growth

this on the economy and the environment are demonstrated in the increased use of raw materials and energy, which causes various ecological problems, and the overall cost of constant replacement, which decreases the population's prosperity. When a shoddy product breaks, it is thrown away and replaced with a new one. Energy and raw materials were expended in the initial production of the item; there now is further expense involved in the destruction or recycling of the broken piece. In addition, replacing the item starts the entire cycle of waste and destruction over again, particularly if the replacement is of similar poor quality.

Each time an individual has to replace an item of poor quality, the amount of money that is available to purchase a different product is reduced. The person either cannot buy the second item or is required to work additional hours in order to afford both the replacement and the new product.

Low-quality products thus destroy both the environment and the potential for prosperity. There are many who argue that this method of production creates millions of jobs for people, jobs that provide the money to purchase the products that are available. Their contention is that if we did not have this type of economic cycle, people would be out of work. They further believe that the production of high-quality products with a long life span would result in unemployment from the manufacturing industry, creating widespread poverty.

Economic activities are meant to serve the people and increase their prosperity, not the other way around. People should not be enslaved by the economy. The chapters explaining the fundamentals and concepts of environomics will show the fallacy of the currently popular and widely held concept.

Another misconception regarding economic growth and prosperity is the increased use of technology, either poorly developed or erroneously applied. Although there is no doubt that technology has made life easier in many regards, there is some question as to its contribution to the general prosperity in real terms and the damage it has done to the environment. The following examples are taken from the Middle Eastern country of Iran. Although there are many examples available from a variety of nations and cultures, these particular examples clearly point out the erroneous application of "modern" technology in Third World countries and are instances with which the author is very familiar.

The Middle East has always suffered from a shortage of water, and Iran is no exception. However, the Iranians generated water for irrigation purposes by employing the oldest method in the world, an ancient practice called "Kanat." Kanat involved digging a series of vertical wells a certain distance apart and horizontally connecting each well to the next until a stream of water started to flow. Starting from the bed of a mountain, this series of wells continued until a valley or flat area of land was reached. The water would surface on the land where it was flattest. Using this method, the villages that grew around the area could cultivate fruits and vegetables. Because the original source of Kanat usually was a spring somewhere in the mountain, a permanent flow of water was maintained. When it was connected to the next well, the water bubbled up and created a stronger stream of water, continuing to the last well. Each Kanat provided water on a permanent basis for several hundred years with no trouble, as long as the passage of water was maintained.

Kanat required maintenance at least once or twice a year. The mud falling into the stream had to be cleaned out to enable the flow of water to continue to the valley; this required work and cost money. Then, the Americans appeared and showed the Iranians how to pull the water out of the ground by using pumps. This method was immediately installed, and the Kanats were allowed to dry out. Unfortunately, the modern methods were less reliable than the Kanats. The motors caused new problems. The engines broke down, parts were unavailable, and fuel supplies were insufficient. In addition, the new wells dried up faster than the people could develop replacement wells, and it was becoming impossible to provide water on a permanent basis.

The farmlands began to dry out, and the farmers were forced to leave their villages and move to the big cities to make a living. The cities became overpopulated, and the once self-sufficient country was forced to import primary agricultural goods as their population moved from rural areas and pursuits. Tehran is considered one of the most populous, and one of the most environmentally damaged, cities in the world.

Politics, both governmental and corporate, have a major effect on the economy and environment. Wealth and power are controlled by a very few individuals around the world. These groups work in their own best interests to generate continued financial benefits and control without contributing to the financial well-being of the general population.

The automobile and fuel to run it is an excellent example. Although there have been some attempts to use other types of fuel, such as alcohol, the fact remains that currently, every car owner is required to periodically purchase fuel in order to use the car for transportation. The immediate results of this are air pollution, exploitation of another natural resource, and reduction in the amount of money an individual has available to spend on other items. There has been periodic talk of other methods of propelling transportation vehicles and minor exploration into energy alternatives in the interest of eliminating our reliance on oil. However, the providers of the fuel have created for themselves and their company an ongoing income, for cars have become a necessity to much of the world's population. In spite of the damage done to the environment, the providers are not anxious to reduce or eliminate their income.

In the late 1970s, interest and experimentation in the solar industry picked up briefly because of a tax credit initiated by the Carter administration. Big corporations like Exxon, Grumman, Olin, and others initially got involved, but their efforts halted abruptly when the tax credit expired. Solar energy as a business required a great deal of research and investment and did not appear to be a source of major income. Regardless of the consequences to the environment, politicians and corporations returned to the guaranteed income from fuel oil and other natural resources that were already proven moneymakers.

Erroneous approaches to energy production of another sort can be demonstrated by our current reliance on artificial methods of cooling our homes. Looking again at an ancient practice of Iran, we could learn much from history. People used to build a tower 30 to 40 feet high, leading to a hall. The tower was called a "wind grapper" and was designed with a square shape divided so that it could capture air from every direction through an opening at the highest level of the tower. When the air came into the tower, it was directed downward. As the heat escaped from the upper part of the opening, the hall started to cool off. In summer months when the temperature would reach 110 degrees Fahrenheit, the hall was cool, retaining a comfortable temperature of 70 to 75 degrees. This environmentally friendly method, which required practically no cost to maintain summer comfort, was replaced with the modern air-conditioning system. In spite of its many benefits and the convenience it provides, it also causes a great deal of damage to the environment, especially the ozone layer around the earth, because of the increased use and discharge of chemicals, such as chlorofluorocarbons, into the atmosphere.

These examples provide some clear idea of the negative effects of our current practices on natural resources and, consequently, prosperity. These and similar matters might have been of insignificant consequence if the range of activities had remained in limits. However, we have routinely ignored our responsibility to our planet, disregarded the effects of the human being on the environment, and exploited the earth and its resources with no thought to the future or the impact on nature.

In the beginning, it was not as critical, because there were few of us to cause destruction. Now, however, the population is exploding, and more and more nations are striving toward industrialization, employing methods and technologies that are highly destructive. At the same time, other nations are trying simply to survive and, in their primitive efforts, are contributing further to the damage of the environment.

The concept and principles of environomics are designed to end the perpetual cycle that threatens the future of both our planet and our population. Appropriate use of technology, use of alternate sources of energy, and application of economic approaches that will contribute to the prosperity of all nations and peoples are not impossible and do not require deprivation or inconvenience.

4

The Fundamentals of Environomics and Redefining Prosperity

Given the proposed positive results, some may expect the fundamentals of environomics to be totally unfamiliar and difficult to understand or implement. This is not the case; the fundamentals require implementing economic measures in the proper way and registering economic developments accurately. The concept requires certain modifications of conventional economic attitudes and approaches and supplementation of existing theories.

Now that we have identified and discussed the major problems that plague both our economy and our environment, let us begin with the basics, the areas in which our economic activities take place. In the four primary areas of allocation of resources, production, distribution, and consumption, anything we do in any one area has some effect on the ecology of the planet, the natural resources available, and the economy of the population. The outcome of activity in these four areas will decide the level of general prosperity and the health of the planet earth. In order to better understand the interrelationship among them, we will explore the origins and nature of each separate issue throughout this work, beginning with allocation.

The major portion of the problems involved in the allocation of resources results from the uneven distribution of raw materials throughout the world. When a country that needs the materials does not have them, the countries in possession of the resource(s) sell them in order to survive. A perfect example of how this situation can get out of control is seen in the crude oil industry, a worldwide situation resulting from our extreme dependence on oil.

Although the oil crisis has severe effects on the prosperity of the majority of the population, the problem is primarily political. Despite this fact, the allocation of crude oil has created severe ecological problems, from the initial stages of exploration and exploitation through the final stage of transport. The problem of which we are most aware, of course, is the contamination of our oceans as a result of offshore drilling operations and oil spills that occur during the transportation of the oil or at the time it is pumped from the ships. We have all seen the pictures and read the news about the damage done to birds, fish, plants, and entire stretches of beaches, damage that has occurred at various points in the exploration for and production of oil.

The destruction of our few remaining rain forests is another clear example of destruction of our natural resources and, at the same time, our existence. During the 1970s, many of the developing countries borrowed money heavily, when prices were high and world trade burgeoned. Recession then set in, and oil prices collapsed. The developing countries faced a collective debt of $1.3 trillion. At the same time, the population explosion in these countries accounted for 82 percent of the world's people.

The poverty and lack of means by which to satisfy basic needs, combined with the desperate drive for mere survival, forced the people of these rapidly growing countries to sell their natural resources or, in some cases, to use them in any manner that would ensure survival. In many cases, the trees of tropical rain forests were cut down to satisfy a portion of the debt, to generate some type of income, or to provide land for cultivation. This uncontrolled act of destruction has created a severe imbalance in the health of the entire planet.

Clearing trees in the tropical rain forest and selling them as timber to industrial nations for quick cash may come to an abrupt end, not through humanity's efforts but through nature's workings. Trees, quite simply, cannot grow as fast as they have been cut down, and in many cases, new trees were not planted to replace the others. Often, tropical rain forest land is used for pasture land or to grow crops. In either case, the land is quickly depleted, and ranchers abandon the fields, cutting down more forest for new pastures.

Few people realize that the deforestation of the tropical rain forests affects more than the balance of oxygen on the planet. This wholesale logging of the areas in question has caused a number of other problems, including the spread of a drier climate over the remaining forest area, causing the forest to shrink and the desert area to grow.

Although nature is responsible for the uneven distribution of raw materials, humanity is responsible for the destruction that has resulted. The lack of insight on the part of our politicians in resolving the allocation problem has caused implementation of a number of policies that have done more harm than good. In attempting to reallocate the natural resources, we are all involved in the process of destruction, the depletion of the sources of raw materials, and the deterioration of the environment, whether our involvement is physical or economic. It matters little whether these actions are due to greed, the exploitation of others, or a simple struggle for survival. Destruction is destruction, regardless of how or why it occurs, and the effects are far-reaching and long-lasting.

The only solution to this vicious circle of destruction is for the richer nations to look into alternatives and apply more rational approaches to the production processes, as discussed later in this book. In addition, these countries must help the poorer nations move away from their desperation and poverty. We must realize that the survival of the people of the rich nations of the world depends a great deal on the methods of survival that must be used by the people of the small nations. If the poor nations, in their struggle to survive, destroy the foundation of our environment — and thus our existence — does it matter how rich the other nations are? Can the rich nations preach and teach to a country whose people are involved in a daily struggle merely to survive? In the ancient Zoroastrian philosophies, priority is given to the body rather than the soul: "First comes the body, then the soul." Until we have assured the survival of the first, the second will not be a consideration.

The second area of economic activities is production, an area in which we have made some of our worst mistakes. Not only have we failed to satisfy the basic needs of the people from an economic standpoint, we also have caused devastating environmental problems.

Consider the causes of acid rain. Although the process is, in fact, quite complex, the basic procedure of burning coal and oil creates sulfur oxides, which the sun then converts into acids. These acids are distributed upon the earth through the raindrops, snowflakes, fogs, and mists or clouds of dust and gas, killing the trees and contaminating the lakes and oceans that are home to fish and seafood.

Another example is the nuclear power plants disposing of their highly contaminated radioactive wastes by placing them in salt mines or under the oceans. The containers in which this waste is stored are subject to damage. In addition, the cooling techniques of the nuclear plants contribute to the atmospheric imbalances through the global warming trend, referred to as the "greenhouse effect."

Chemical plants can be considered a third example, causing damage to the ecology and the living creatures in rivers and oceans by dumping their poisonous wastes into nearby waterways. One of these deadly poisons is mercury, a heavy liquid metal used in several industries. This is being dispersed through burning, dumping, and spraying, affecting the air, the water, and even our food. Companies that produce chlorine, plastics, and paper items add to the pollution of lakes, rivers, and bays by dumping the mercury or mercury compounds used during production.

As these examples clearly demonstrate, we pollute our air, water, and land throughout the production process. This is not a good method of producing goods and energy to begin with, but the problem is intensified by the fact that we must continually produce the same product, over and over. The general endeavor of the industrial world is the production of a given number of items in a shorter time or an increase in the number of products made within the same time. If either of these goals is accomplished, the contention is that productivity has increased quantitatively, a positive accomplishment. Such a concept is absurd, and it is this type of thinking that must be reformed. Our production methods are far from being safe for the environment, and they do not have any positive impact on the majority of the population. They are, in fact, extremely destructive. When we speed up the production process to produce more goods in a shorter period, thus using our raw materials at a faster rate, we are galloping toward our own extinction. We must reverse this approach and attempt to accomplish production in a positive way.

There are many who espouse the belief that the application of recycling methods during the production process will help solve many of the problems created by the process. We have heard this from the so-called experts through the popular media. However, recycling solves only those portions of the problem that are concerned with the allocation of raw materials and preventing pollution of the land. The rest of the problems remain, the type of problem and its extensiveness determined by the type of product and the production stages necessary to reach completion. Although recycling is certainly a step in the right direction, it resolves only a fraction of the entire problem.

The solution is to prevent the need for recycling. We need to develop production methods that reduce the requirements for recycling to a minimum level. We need to explore methods that prevent creation of goods that require recycling. The solutions to the ecological and economic problems related to production require a great deal of research and effort.

The part of the economic system that causes the least amount of environmental harm, compared with the other three, is the distribution aspect. Most environmental harm occurs during the allocation and production processes. When it comes to distribution, the major damage is probably related to the packaging of the product and the transportation of goods to the consumers. Recycling allows us to deal with the packaging materials to a large extent. The pollution caused by transporting the goods is, compared with the overall picture, relatively negligible. Again, the major negative aspect is the tremendous use of energy and raw materials.

The environmental damage that results from the consumption or usage of finished products is substantial, occurring in the form of air and water pollution and the creation of incredible amounts of garbage. Although recycling can provide some remedy in dealing with the trash, the matters of air and water pollution are much more difficult to resolve. The primary issue here is the implementation of a series of measures, including changing many of our existing habits and requiring that each and every one of us, whether individuals or corporations, become more conscious of the effect of our actions on the environment. It is critical that we avoid the use of hazardous and pollution-causing products, preventing the pollution caused by cars or the contamination of underground water reservoirs when used petroleum products are handled carelessly or dumped thoughtlessly on the ground. The deterioration of the sewage systems, particularly the effects of using phosphates such as those found in many detergents, is another example. Land pollution is created by burying the land under trash and garbage collected from households and industrial sites.

Recycling our waste materials is, indeed, a part of the solution but is only a very small step toward solving the overall problem. Much more is needed to solve the environmental dilemma we have created. We can see that it is relatively easy to resolve the environmental problems created by distribution and consumption, and there is already tremendous potential for addressing these issues. The major areas of concern, however, the most detrimental areas of the cycle, are the allocation and production processes. If the proper methods and approaches are implemented, most, if not all, of the destruction occurring during these two steps in the economic cycle can also be eliminated. Through the application of environomics, all four areas of economic activity can become less harmful to our environment and therefore to our continued existence on this planet. Even better, general prosperity, in real terms, can be achieved.

Having identified the sources of the environmental problems and the requirements to remedy our mistakes and excesses, the question is how to resolve these issues. Before an answer can be offered, it is necessary to identify the economic problems that have led to the environmental concerns in the first place. Exploring this issue helps provide the answer that will automatically start us in the right direction to create environmentally safe prosperity following the concepts of environomics. One of the major stumbling blocks has been conventional economic theories and approaches.

Understanding the concept of environomics requires an understanding of the crucial questions behind the logic used in calculating the gross national product (GNP). This calculation method includes a number of gaps and several errors in logic.

Among economists, the traditional scorecard for economic progress is the GNP, which supposedly represents the value of the total amount of goods and services produced by a given economy during a given period of time, usually within one year. The GNP is used by almost everyone — economists, politicians, and businessmen — as a measure of national economic conditions. Because of the method of calculating the GNP, this comprehensive usage is a major part of the problem.

Do you know what would happen if when you balanced your checkbook, you added the amount of all the checks written to your balance instead of subtracting the check amounts from the money you started with? You would go broke and create a financial disaster for yourself and problems for anyone to whom you had written checks. Unfortunately, this is a simplified example of how the GNP is calculated by our economists. To further complicate matters, not only are they using an invalid calculation, but much of the data applied in that calculation are very difficult to verify and not always correct. We know that the GNP of a country is not particularly meaningful unless we know the size of the country's population. Our census system attempts to provide that information, but the data are often incorrect and frequently obsolete.

In addition, the GNP does not take into account one of man's most prized activities, leisure, nor does it take adequate account of the changes in the quality of goods as a factor in the final price of the item. It does not reflect the social costs arising from the production of goods and services. The most disturbing issue, however, is the fact that, in calculating the GNP, those items that should be treated as deductions are added in order to boost the numbers. This results in a situation similar to the example of adding checks to your balance instead of deducting them.

There are a number of examples of those items that are added to the GNP erroneously. The bullets we produce — we cannot eat them; the tanks we manufacture — we cannot use them to travel from one place to another; the fighter jets that we develop — we cannot use them as commercial airplanes. The only way these items contribute to the economy is if they are sold to other countries and the money paid for them is used to consume imported goods. This, too, has its limitations. It would work only if a few countries produce these types of goods, export them, and then, with the money earned from the sale, import consumable goods. In addition, this could be successful in the long term only if the nations of this planet were not economically and environmentally interdependent on each other's well-being.

I am not questioning the necessity of national defense, and no one is saying these items should not be produced. The point is, these items should not be added to the GNP but must be subtracted. Similarly, the cost of medical treatment does not increase the wealth of a nation but presents a social cost and should be subtracted from the GNP, not added as a productive product. In reality, all social costs should be subtracted from the GNP, as they impact individual prosperity, the environment, and our natural resources and do not produce any tangible goods.

Replacement costs are added to the GNP when, in reality, they often should be deducted. When a product is sold, that product is expected to last for a certain number of years. If one has an item that has been designed to last for five years and any part of this product breaks, requiring repair or replacement, production of the spare parts is required. We all know this is not an uncommon occurrence. However, why is this considered as an addition to boost the GNP? In actuality, there has been no product manufactured, only parts or pieces to put an existing item back into workable condition. Remember, the value of the product, supposedly based on its usefulness, was calculated into the GNP at the time it was manufactured.

The standard accounting practices applied to the GNP include depreciation, to reflect normal wear and tear, for buildings and equipment. However, two critical issues are neglected or ignored. First, it is assumed that space, raw materials, and energy are infinite. Second, the gradual decline in or prevention of the negative effect this has on the prosperity of the individual or the nation as a whole is not considered.

Pollution is treated as an industry that contributes to the GNP, instead of being more properly considered a cost of growth. Consequently, money spent to clean up catastrophic oil spills boosts the GNP, instead of being considered a cost factor that should be deducted. This is one of the reasons why conventional economic growth is not reconcilable with environmental protection. According to conventional economists and the current manner of viewing the economy, generating pollution increases the national income and then cleaning up that pollution adds further dollars to the total. This is completely opposite what is really happening. Pollution of the environment and cleaning up that pollution are both costs to the population and should not be used to increase the level of the GNP.

Just as water, land, and air must be clean and healthy, we as individuals must be healthy, too. However, this is not the case. As our environment becomes more and more polluted, through our various economic activities, we become sick and injured, many times as a result of the contaminates, pollution, accidents, and such that result from the polluted environmental sources. Maintenance and improvement of our health and treatment for illness and injury are costs.

National defense, health care, police protection, pollution control devices, the cleanup of ecological problems, repairs and replacement of poorly made cars and appliances — none of these should be added during the calculation of the GNP. A large part of our labor force, those staffing the myriad bureaucracies of the federal, state, and local governments, as well as those of the corporate world, function in areas in which their performances must realistically be considered as unproductive and therefore be deducted from true production, which is consumable.

The difference between these two different economic activities is, or should be, considered as the net national product (NNP) and should reflect what is available for disposition. This is a much more logical calculation than the current method of simply deducting estimated depreciation from the GNP to reach the NNP. If we continue to engage ourselves more and more in destructive processes and repair on one side while overspending ourselves on the other side, the health — if not the actual existence — of our economy and ecology will be lost. What is required is a scaling down of the GNP and the economy, one that reflects the real and actual picture. Through realization of this step, we would have a much better idea of the extent of productive goods and services actually available for disposition and consumption.

We have to first distinguish between true cost and income to figure out how much is really available. The current method of calculating the GNP does not provide an accurate picture of the nation's economic well-being. As impressive as our GNP numbers may appear, they are illusory, and when realistically considered, the GNP is much smaller than we believe.

The intention of the U.S. Department of Commerce to emphasize the gross domestic product (GDP), instead of the GNP, for measuring the economy's performance does not address this issue either. Both measurements gauge the total output of goods and services. The GNP is calculated on production by U.S. residents, regardless of location; the GDP measures production within the nation's borders. Whether using the GNP or GDP, the erroneous calculation method is employed and the same problems and misleading numbers result.

By presenting the problems with the GNP, it is hoped that we will not only draw attention to the current implications but also make it easier to understand the concept of environomics, by providing the basis for the existing situation and offering a method of comparison.

What is the relationship between the GNP and prosperity? In fact, what is prosperity or what should one imagine under the word "prosperity"? The dictionary defines "prosperity" as "success . . . a period of well-being." Whenever economists talk about prosperity, their attention is systematically drawn to the GNP of a particular nation, its economic growth, welfare situation, quality of life, and, finally, standard of living. All of this taken together gives an indication of the level of the prosperity of that nation and its people.

The subject is highly controversial, as are the definitions and assumptions regarding prosperity. What documents a higher level of prosperity in one country, as compared with another? The word "prosperity" is very vague and can be interpreted and envisioned differently, with a wide range of economic advantages. The intention of this work is to provide guidelines for achieving an environmentally safe prosperity, a prosperity such as outlined below.

The very first step toward prosperity is reaching that level at which everyone, from the day of birth to the day of death, has access to life's basics — food, clothing, housing, health care, a safe, clean, and enjoyable environment. In addition, energy and the potential for transportation should be available. Prosperity means that in the course of having access to these basics, no one should be made to suffer either physically or mentally; no one should have to work so many hours that there is no time left for family or leisure. Stress and overwork do not constitute well-being.

A heightened level of prosperity would include items such as a home, car, television, or other more luxurious products. Although these are currently expensive to obtain, they belong in a comfortable and worry-free lifestyle, and people should be able to buy and enjoy them in the younger years of their life. As people get older, they should be economically well-off with debts paid, putting them in a position to work less and enjoy more leisure time. The ultimate height of prosperity occurs when the individual has reached the point where all economic needs are taken care of and the requirement for work is reduced. In simplistic terms, the less a person needs to work to satisfy economic requirements and the more leisure time available, the higher is the level of prosperity. When individuals have more time to pursue the things they enjoy, their quality of life improves accordingly.

This should not be confused with wealth, which is based on the accumulation of material goods. Although there is not a unified definition of "quality of life," and different people have different values and ideas, the factors that influence one's quality of life can be identified as direct or indirect. Direct influencing factors include poverty, environmental problems, wars, accidents, and crimes. Indirect factors encompass education, peace, economic and political freedom, and leisure time available. The general prosperity of a nation is achieved when at least a majority of the people have been put into the higher level of prosperity.

To many, this description of prosperity — everyone having the basics that they need — may sound like a utopian society, something we are far from having at present. However, by understanding and implementing the following concepts and practices, the realization of this type of life is not only possible, but also not that difficult to attain. Regardless of the term applied to this type of society, the people of the world would enjoy an environmentally safe, general prosperity.

Once we have corrected our way of thinking in regard to the existing economic misconceptions, such as the calculation of the GNP, we need to employ a series of measures to build the foundation of environomics. The current theories and debates on economics have resulted from contributions made by great economic thinkers, past and present. Unfortunately, these individuals lacked vision in considering the limits set by our natural resources and the environment, and they lacked the foresight to resolve the economic problems contained within the areas of production and allocation. These people concentrated on the monetary, fiscal cycles. Although most of the conventional economic theories have served a purpose, during this age of declining natural resources and drastically deteriorating ecology, these theories and concepts are not capable of addressing the problems created through the escalating pressures for a safe and healthy environment in combination with improvement of the general prosperity. In this regard, there is no difference between the different schools of thought within the field of economics, whether classical, Keynesian, Marxist, monetarist, or supply-sider.

Now that we know where the economic and environmental problems originate and how they are caused, we need to explore the ways to make corrections and adjustments in every area of our economic activity, especially production, in order to achieve the desired result.

One of the prevailing misconceptions held by economists, politicians, and industrialists is the belief in and practice of manufacturing products with a short life span and limited durability and simply producing more of them. This belief is based on the theory that the combination of these two factors, which results in the production of more goods than produced in the previous period of production, represents growth (quantitative growth, of course).

To boost productivity, techniques and production processes are improved so we can manufacture these goods even faster and produce higher quantities in the same period of time. The GNP then is calculated, using the method described earlier, and it appears to be larger than ever, justifying the division of the economic booty into ever-larger shares. We are told that this process, applied during the production phase of economic activity, reduces unemployment and inflation because of the abundance of goods and thereby creates prosperity.

If the continuation of this process is disturbed, the Keynesians prescribe fiscal intervention; the monetarists suggest that regulation of the money volume would help to restore the ideal situation; the supply-siders offer another version of fiscal intervention; and the Marxists are primarily interested in dividing the pie, rather than in producing.

Where does the environmental aspect and the issue of limited natural resources fit into these conventional economic thoughts and philosophies? Nowhere! The fact is that this method of production is exploitive and destructive and can lead only to dead ends, as we are becoming more and more aware. Not only do we exploit and destroy our fossil energy and our natural resources, we also do the same to our environment and our economy. How can individuals prosper, when they are continually replacing products for which they recently paid? Or worse, replacing products for which they are still paying?

There is no question that the economies of the former East Bloc countries are in trouble, floundering in disarray. Why? Many subscribe to the theory that it is because of the inferiority of the centrally planned economic system, as compared with the more positive features of the market-oriented economy. Although there may be some truth to this — very few would deny the positive features of the market-oriented system — the main problem lies in the inferior methods of production in those countries, resulting in finished products that are inferior to those in the West. How can the people of a nation expect to prosper if they have to repair or replace purchased items on a regular basis, often before the original item has been paid for? The opportunity for prosperity is severely reduced under these circumstances, and the negative effects on the environment and our natural resources cannot be overlooked.

How do we improve this situation? How do we prevent arbitrary exploitation and exhaustion of raw materials and fossil energy sources, protect the environment, and still contribute to the general prosperity of the people? The answer is relatively simple and probably reflects thoughts and feelings you have expressed in this regard. The answer is to change our thinking and our priorities from quantitative growth to qualitative growth.

Environomics maximizes the positive effects of economic activity on prosperity and the environment while minimizing negative impact. Goods and services must be produced and offered in a manner that contributes to general prosperity rather than leading to poverty through hidden inflation. To achieve this goal, the myth of quantitative economic growth must be replaced with qualitative growth, which is brought about by increasing the useful life of goods. This reduces the necessity of people having to work for the sole purpose of maintaining a standard of living — earning money that is required to replace, repair, or finance goods. Gradually, as each household achieves greater prosperity with fewer hours of work, more jobs would be freed up for new workers. In addition, global demand for quality goods would more than replace any decline in the United States' domestic demand, resulting from improved products with increased life spans.

We have already discussed quantitative growth — producing more products faster, products with limited quality and a short life span. Qualitative growth is achieved when the goods produced have a longer life expectancy, when they are more durable than before. If we produce more products with longer life expectancies and increased durability in a given period of time, we have truly increased productivity. Also, if we increase the actual durability and useful life span of a product, we have helped to increase the prosperity of the user, because we have extended the time that elapses before additional money has to be spent on repair or replacement. This means we have made available additional disposable income for the purchase of other goods, thereby increasing the standard of living for the individual.

If the individual does not want additional products, the number of working hours necessary to support the current standard of living can be reduced and the amount of leisure time can be increased. This situation represents true prosperity.

What would be the effect of qualitative growth on the environment? In fact, it would require fewer destructive economic activities, both individually and collectively, to satisfy economic needs. As a result there would be less environmental damage and reduced depletion of fossil energy and natural resources. Thinking in terms of qualitative growth is the first step.

In manufacturing products, especially industrial items, we employ technology to ease the process. Our approach to technology is critical, both for the reconciliation of economic activities and for the environment.

In order to understand the appropriate use of technology, it is necessary to distinguish between three types of goods.

First are the primary goods, which include all kinds of raw materials, such as iron and copper ores, crude oil, and uranium. Next are the secondary goods, items such as heating oil, electricity, and partially finished products, like plastics, which are later used to make specific items. Finally there are the finished products, items like homes, cars, and televisions — actual items that we buy and use. We have discussed switching from quantitative growth to qualitative growth by increasing the life span and durability of finished products, in order to save and protect our raw materials, our environment, and our disposable income. An equally critical factor, crucial in helping us to achieve general prosperity and create a safe environment, is changing the direction of our thoughts on technology. Current technologies are neither sound nor desirable when viewed from the standpoint of the environment and general prosperity. We must distinguish between two types of technologies, prosperity-inducing technology (PIT) and prosperity-decreasing technology (PDT).

Some people categorize technologies as being either harmful or benign. This is a step in the right direction but not precise enough to determine their effect on the environment and the economy. A benign technology may be harmless to the environment but may not induce prosperity. Harmful technologies not only affect the environment adversely, they also have negative effects on the prosperity. For this reason, PIT and PDT provide a better way to define technologies in terms of environomics.

It is imperative that we make increasing use of the PITs, which are environmentally safe and induce prosperity, while avoiding the use of PDTs, which have the opposite result. However, the way a technology is employed can provide all the features of PIT without contributing directly to prosperity.

Windmills and solar energy are a clear case of employing PITs that do not pollute the environment and cost practically nothing to operate. However, a difference occurs when such methods are employed through centralized (versus decentralized) power plants. If the energy is produced on a large scale and, through centralized power plants, supplied to the consumer at no cost, they fulfill the requirements of a PIT to the largest extent. The technology is environmentally safe and helps to induce the prosperity of the consumers by eliminating the need to pay for electricity. As a result, the consumer has that amount of money available each month to purchase other products. If the consumers have to pay for the energy generated by these plants, they at least have an indirect fiscal advantage in that they do not have to pay the social costs associated with the power plants using PDT. This approach, however, is not prosperity inducing. On the other hand, the use of windmills and solar energy in small, individual, decentralized power systems would totally fulfill the prerequisites of a PIT.

Nuclear power plants and plants powered by oil and coal to generate electricity are true examples of PDTs, those technologies that pollute the environment and employ techniques that decrease prosperity as a whole. Not only are consumers required to pay for the electricity every month, but individuals also pay indirectly for the associated costs of cleaning up the pollution created during the process.

Another example that demonstrates the possibility of employing PIT or PDT by one and the same kind of product is the automobile. For instance, a solar-powered car is based on PIT. It does not pollute the environment, and it costs nothing to drive. By comparison, a gas-powered car is based on PDT, causing pollution and costing money to run.

Unfortunately, there are very few signs of individuals, corporations, or nations employing PITs, and we are just at the beginning stage of developing these types of technology. To protect the environment and induce prosperity, we must move rapidly and consistently toward employing the PITs and eliminating PDTs. Accordingly, we have to move toward developing and using products based on PITs. The sooner we get away from the PDTs and adapt the PITs, the sooner we will begin protecting our environment and increasing our prosperity.

Using anything to excess brings dependency, particularly if there are problems with the availability or implementation. The best example of this is crude oil. The same dependency problem could occur with technology, if it has not already. A dangerous potential can be seen in the increased and arbitrary use of nuclear energy technology. It is to be hoped that as we are at the early stage of converting from PDTs to PITs, this dependency does not occur.

A total independence from technology is impossible, from a practical standpoint, but strategies could be employed that would reduce the level of that dependence. For example, it is imperative that we move away from the centralized use of PITs and employ decentralized approaches, especially in the area of energy production. A centralized power plant can affect an entire area, should there be a breakdown at the plant, whereas the breakdown of hundreds of smaller, decentralized plants would have a relatively insignificant impact. The ideal situation would be for every house, building, factory, or other facility to generate their own power needs using plants based on PIT. Although this may sound illusory, it is not at all unrealistic.

Sharp critics may arise who perceive a lack of sensitivity or vision for technological progress in the concept of environomics, particularly in the recommended switch from quantitative to qualitative growth described in this work. There may be some concern that by increasing the life span and durability of a product, the product will become obsolete during its lifetime, from the standpoint of technological progress. Continued technological advances could even create a new generation of the product. This is a valid concern; however, a key part of the concept of environomics recommends that different parts of products should be developed in modular form, thus allowing new technology to be incorporated into the existing product by simply snapping out the obsolete parts and snapping in the newer ones. This approach contributes to the maintenance of the state-of-the-art technology in existing products without adding further to the environmental problems by using raw materials and energy to create a completely new product. Again, prosperity would be induced, as individuals would purchase only the updated modular part. The necessity of purchasing an entire product is eliminated. Because progress in technology generally takes place in such a manner that only a part of the product is affected, this type of modular approach is the most effective way of maintaining a durable product.

By following the concept of environomics, we can protect our precious natural resources and our environment. This approach would also contribute to the improvement of our prosperity. As a result, there would be a substantial improvement in the quality of life for each and every individual.

5

Expanding and Refining the Principles of Environomics

The principles of environomics are amazingly simply and easily applicable, yet often difficult for the majority of people to understand and implement. To the best of my knowledge, there is not a single book available among existing literature that deals with the topic of enviroeconomic problems and provides a comprehensive and applicable approach such as the one offered here. Environomics can be seen in two aspects of this book.

First, in environomics, not only are the ideas and concepts regarding technology further developed, but also an effort has been made to refine its function in resolving the environmental problems and contributing to a general prosperity through the introduction and definition of terms such as "prosperity-inducing technology" (PIT) and "prosperity-decreasing technology" (PDT). We also have introduced terms such as "modular design," as applied to the development of products, and will explain the necessity of "decentralized modular energy systems."

Further, environomics has provided definitions for terms such as "qualitative growth" and its measurement, as economic indicators in the manufacturing and service sectors, to show changes in the level of general prosperity, "quality," "productivity by qualitative growth," and "quality of life." Of course, no claim is made for the completeness of this coverage, as more research must follow. However, this is the first attempt to get a grip on the actual meanings behind these principles and present them in proper context.

Some of the principles presented in environomics need more detailed explanation in order to cover the important aspects of the subject. Others need to be brought into the context of historical development in order to realize the significance of the definitions provided in environomics. Here, we will attempt to elaborate, expand, and refine the concepts of environomics.

QUALITATIVE GROWTH

Since the early 1970s, when the social-economic structure of the industrial world started to show a rift as a result of the oil crisis and the rising conscience of the people regarding the environmental problems, a transitional solution was thought to be the replacement of quantitative growth with qualitative growth. It was determined that this would prevent the exploitation and exhaustion of our natural resources and provide protection for the environment. However, in spite of a variety of conferences and the involvement of national and international institutions and organizations, no one could come up with a definition or description that would provide an applicable solution. The theory had no substance, and because of various ideas regarding what qualitative growth really was, the entire concept was vague.

The initial discussion regarding the environment and natural resources was triggered in 1972, when Dennis L. Meadows' book *The Limits to Growth* was published. Although the world public exhibited a great deal of interest in this subject and got involved in the discussion, the primary interest was exhibited by the Germans. Their increased interest may have been due, to some extent, to the smallness of their country and the lack of substantial raw materials, but it is believed that the Greenpeace movement, which began in that country, contributed a great deal to the conscience of the Germans in regard to environmental matters.

As a result of this, academia developed a great interest in the subject, as did the different political groups and parties who were entering the discussion. By studying different literature regarding the environmental issue, it seems the Germans have devoted more time to investigating this area and have made more progress toward positive approaches to the environment than have other countries. The Germans have already given serious thought to reducing the weekly working hours, an environmentally friendly measure, while in the United States the trend seems to be going the opposite way. Of more concern is the fact that the interest in saving or protecting the environment seems to have lost momentum in the United States.

In spite of their achievements, the Germans have not yet effectively solved the problem, particularly the issue of qualitative growth, nor have others who have studied the issue. A great number of authors and political institutions have different visions of what this term means. Gottfried Bombach delivered one definition at the International Conference of the IG Metall, a German labor union. The contention was that in order to achieve a qualitative growth, it was necessary that the share of public goods and services in the GNP be substantially increased and the share of consumptive goods be reduced accordingly. The German's Social Democratic Party contends that qualitative growth can be seen in the improvement of working conditions under ecological aspects. Herbert Gruhl, a member of the German Parliament and one of the most famous German environmentalists, qualifies qualitative growth as an increase in the GNP that has been achieved without using either increased energy or raw materials, assuming this was accomplished with no adverse effects on the ecology.

There are many who define qualitative growth as a compromise between quantitative growth and the radical environmental strategy. Others find qualitative growth identical with quality of life. However, the improvement of the quality of life is measured by the potential for each individual to freely determine and participate in social and economic activities and events, as well as political activities and events. True improvement in quality of life would result in each individual enjoying an equal opportunity to share in these three areas.

The definition from the Organization for Economic Cooperation and Development (OECD) views the achievements in areas of social welfare as quality of life. Social welfare includes health care, education, work and the quality of working life, leisure, economic situation, living environment, social environment, social opportunities and social participation, personal security, legal rights, and the political system.

All these and other differing definitions can be condensed down to an improvement of material needs, social needs, environmental needs, cultural needs, and political needs. The main question, however, remains. How do we accomplish all these praiseworthy goals? To date, no satisfactory or effective answer has been given.

There is no doubt that satisfying the basic human needs, as mentioned before, has priority over satisfying any other economic needs. People need something to eat, clothes to wear, a place to live, and the ability to move around before other needs can be considered or given priority. This necessitates that goods and services be made available to an overwhelming majority of the population, if not to all of them.

In a world where there are more people seeking goods than there are goods in existence, it may sound absurd to strive toward zero-growth production. However, the view is not so absurd if it concentrates on *quantitative* zero growth; qualitatively, there must be indefinite growth. There may be cases in which it will be necessary to produce a larger number or quantity of goods to satisfy the growing number of people who will be able to afford them, items like homes or health care devices, for example.

In a country with zero population growth that has satisfied its population's material needs to a great extent, a policy of quantitative zero growth does not preclude qualitative growth. Theoretically, it is possible that at some point that particular country would not need to produce any more products for a given period of time, if a saturation of demand is reached. However, in the real world, no country consumes all the products it manufactures, but exports a certain amount of those products. Still, if a country is growing qualitatively and meeting the requirements of qualitative growth, there should be no need for quantitative growth. Should there be brief periods when quantitative growth appears necessary, it must be accomplished within the specifications of qualitative growth.

The following is a simplistic example. Assume a country produces one car a year and that car is built to last for only one year. There are three people in the country who are to be provided with cars. Every year, when a car is produced, it must be used to replace the car from the previous year. The result is that two people never get a car. If the life span of the car is increased from one year to two years, two of the three people will always be getting the cars, yet the continued demand for the car will exist. On the other hand, if the life span of the car is increased to three years, within three years all of the people will have a car. In this situation, the production level will still have to be kept the same in order to satisfy the car needs of these three people, due to replacement requirements. If the life span of the car is increased to four years, not only will the needs of these three people be satisfied, but also there will be a car available to export to other nations. Although the numbers are much larger and more complicated in real life, this example shows the result of channeling production in the right direction and recognizing responsibilities toward the environment and the economy.

Some may question which products should grow and which should not grow or even be eliminated. Following the concept of environomics, there should be no question that those industrial products that feature PIT and other principles of environomics, which are environmentally friendly and prosperity inducing, should continue to develop and qualitatively grow, as long as there is a demand and the market absorbs them. The market demand would determine which goods should be produced, just as it does now.

However, the production and usage of products and technologies featuring PDTs must be totally phased out as soon as possible. Whatever the type of product or technology employed, it is critical that it exhibit the features of the principles of environomics.

If qualitative growth must be accompanied by quantitative growth (required for immediate satisfaction of needs), how does one address this situation? If quantitative growth destroys and exhausts the natural resources and causes damage to the environment, will not the same thing happen when qualitative growth is achieved quantitatively? Because quantitative growth, or numeric increase of qualitative growth, is necessary to satisfy the needs, the damages to the environment and to natural resources would be limited — even relatively negligible — if this is achieved by employing the concept of environomics. Qualitative growth, increased quantitatively, would help satisfy given economic needs in a shorter time span, assuming that the related technology has reached the height of its development.

In order to make this point clear, let us assume that qualitative growth has been achieved by a given product or technology by increasing its life span and durability from 10 years to 20 years. Although this indicates an increase qualitatively, if the production of this item or technology is increased quantitatively, it could be qualified as quantitative growth in a later calculation of the GNP. As long as quantitative growth of a product or technology is achieved *after* the item has reached its maximum qualitative growth, the quantitative growth would have few, if any, damaging effects on the environment and natural resources. Quantitative growth under these specifications would contribute to an increase in general prosperity.

Critics may question whether the price of a product with a longer life span and increased durability would be substantially higher. Would it not require more energy and raw materials for its production? If so, how could this have a positive effect on the environment, save energy and raw materials, and contribute to the general prosperity? We have no reason to assume that production of a superior product would require more raw material or energy than production of an inferior product. Even if initial costs were higher, the savings in raw materials and energy over the long run would be substantially less if, for instance, the product lasted twice as long and did not cost double to produce.

Suppose we double the life span of an automobile from five years to ten years by manufacturing a car that is much more durable and dependable than the current models. Let us further assume that the cost of the extra materials and energy is 30 percent over the current production costs. If a superior car costs $13,000, as compared with the inferior car that costs $10,000, and the life span and durability of the superior car are double that of the inferior one, the superior car is 77 percent cheaper to buy. In this instance, you would spend $13,000 once in ten years, as opposed to spending $10,000 twice in ten years — a $13,000 expenditure instead of a total $20,000 expenditure. In addition to the purchase price comparison, one must consider the financing costs associated with buying the second car.

The environmental costs reflect a similar comparison. Even if more material and energy were required for the superior car, they would be required only once in ten years, not twice. There can be little doubt that the environmental damage caused by manufacturing two inferior cars is higher than that resulting from the production of one car.

The final consideration is the fact that purchase of one superior car in ten years would improve the personal finances of an individual. How can qualitative growth be measured and what can be used as an indicator? Perhaps the best economic indicator for measuring the qualitative growth of a product is the manufacturer's warranty promises and performance. The longer the period of warranty and the more extensive the manufacturer's coverage provided by the warranty, the greater the indication of a quality product. No manufacturer is going to provide a comprehensive and long-term warranty on a product that will require a great deal of repair; to do so would result in losing money servicing the warranty repairs. However, if a product is of high quality and built for durability, the manufacturer can easily provide a strong warranty, a guarantee of quality.

Even when efforts are made to provide top quality, there will be instances when a product requires repair. Because of this fact, it is in the manufacturer's best interest to assure that warranty repairs and replacements can be made in a cost-effective manner. The longer the length of the warranty and the more comprehensive its coverage, the more important it becomes for the manufacturer to provide for repairs during the designing and manufacturing of the product in question. This is an example of the rational behavior that is required to attain the goals of environomics.

When warranty coverage is limited and the length of that coverage is short-term, there is little incentive for providing ease of repair. A poor-quality product, available for a cheap price, usually has limited durability, and it is often easier to replace the item than to pay for repair. In this case, the manufacturer has no concern about cost-effectiveness of repair. When the item breaks, there is a market for a new, replacement item, thus creating the spiral of disposal, waste, and raw material use. Little thought is given to the fact that a high-quality, durable product, designed in such a manner that warranty repairs would be cost-effective and rarely required, would be worth a higher price to the consumer.

Let us examine a practical example of the suggested rational approach to cost-effective warranty replacement. The Chrysler Voyager has, as an option, an electrical side mirror. If there is any type of problem with this mirror, the vehicle owner is forced to replace the entire apparatus — mirror, plastic attachment, housing, and electrical parts. Had Chrysler Corporation made the plastic attachment to the mirror a separate component, with or without the mirror, such total replacement would not be required. If the mirror were shattered, all one would need to do is pop in a new mirror, rather than replace the entire mechanism.

If this approach is so simple, why did Chrysler, and other manufacturers for that matter, not think of it? Profit. The cost of the entire side mirror set is approximately $92 at this writing; the cost of the mirror would be approximately $3. In addition to the cost of parts, there is the income from the labor involved. Needless to say, even though it costs Chrysler more to manufacture the entire mechanism, there is a higher profit in selling and installing the complete replacement part. The only person to whom this is less attractive is the vehicle owner, who must either pay to replace parts that are still usable or manage without the side mirror.

The effects of this irrational behavior extend beyond the unhappy car owner, however. This approach is common in the manufacturing industry and has had devastating effects on the environment, energy resources, raw materials, and the overall economy. These effects cannot be ignored or overlooked.

At best, this tactic temporarily boosts the income and profit of the manufacturing enterprise. At the same time, it has other, more serious negative effects. First, it distorts the real picture presented by the GNP, as was discussed earlier by reflecting a replacement cost as increased value in goods and services produced in the country. This could impact the inflation rate by making it appear that people are purchasing more new goods, sending the population searching for what appears to be new manufacturing, distribution, and sales. However, the GNP is not reflecting any new goods or service, only the fact that an existing product was put back into its original, working condition.

Had the same incident — a broken side mirror — occurred where an enterprise was operating under the concept of environomics, the result would be quite different. The vehicle would have been covered by a long-term, comprehensive warranty. Because the manufacturer would be responsible for the cost of repair and replacement, it is likely that the parts would have been designed so that components could be quickly and inexpensively repaired or replaced, thus limiting the service liability under the warranty. In this scenario, it is more probable that repair of the broken side mirror would require nothing more intricate than slipping the $3 replacement part into the housing.

The positive results would be multiple. Because the necessity of replacing an entire mechanism was removed, there would be considerably less waste of raw materials and energy resources. The consumer would have $89 in available disposable income. Based on a reputation for quality and service, the manufacturer would have a sound income and healthy profit picture. Although it is true that there would be fewer return buyers, that is, individuals who were forced to replace their vehicles, there would be more new buyers, as quality products freed the consumer to purchase new, instead of replacement, products. As the concept of environomics is applied universally, the domestic consumers would be joined by foreign consumers. Following these guidelines, the enterprise would maintain a steady, healthy economic position, a positive improvement over the recent ups and downs in the auto industry that have resulted in plant closings and widespread unemployment in certain areas of our country.

Given the example above, it is clear that integrated components and modular design must be integrated into the manufacturing process; this is one of the basic elements of environomics. As quality improves, there will be less need for repair of broken parts. However, there will be an increased requirement to replace obsolete parts as technology develops. Today's approach usually requires replacement of the entire product or, at the least, replacement of parts that are not obsolete in order to eliminate those that are. Again, this is done to enhance the profit of the manufacturer and creates a false picture of the economy through the GNP while serving a detrimental blow to the environment and the consumer. Products must be designed in such a manner that only the technologically obsolete part requires replacement to make the entire item functional and up-to-date.

As the principles of higher-quality manufacturing, modular design, and ease of repair/replacement are put into practice, measurement of qualitative growth can be accomplished in part by tracking the warranty performance from year to year. Any increase in the warranty performance over that of the previous year could be considered as growth in the quality of that product — qualitative growth. This measurement can be applied to all industrial and consumer goods, allowing the calculation of an average for the year. When that average is divided by the previous year's average, you derive the annual qualitative growth rate.

Warranty performance is not an applicable measurement in the service sector, where different methods must be applied as economic indicators. The goal of the service industries is to perform faster, better, and cheaper within a given time unit. This is very similar to the definition of productivity in this area, which requires that two or more services be provided simultaneously at the same time and/or cost unit. Rarely can warranty performance be used as an indicator to measure this type of qualitative growth.

Once services have been provided — two or more at the same time or cost unit, instead of one — to meet the productivity definition, the only results are that the services were done properly, the services were done improperly, or the services had to be repeated. The satisfaction of the customer is the determination of the quality of the service performed. If services were done to the satisfaction of the customer, with no need to repeat them, there would now be time to offer those services to an expanded group of customers. An increase in productivity growth in the service sector, which leads to increased availability of those services as compared with the previous year, could provide an indication for qualitative growth in that sector. The same calculations for qualitative growth comparison in manufacturing would then apply to the figures.

In many respects, increasing the availability of services to a larger number of people represents quantitative growth in the service sector. However, in this context, qualitative growth is the basis of the quantitative growth, and a combination of the two is necessary to achieve an increased level of general prosperity.

The key issue in qualitative growth is that information regarding qualitative growth in the manufacturing and service sectors can serve as an economic indicator for determining and controlling the condition and extent of achievement in the pursuit of an environmentally safe general prosperity.

What is quality, and why is quality so important? Quality has a wide range of features and it is difficult to find a simple definition for it. The difficulty is compounded by a society that is dominated by quantity. Quality may be characterized by the type of product in question.

When somebody talks about the quality of an industrial product, one usually thinks about the durability and higher life expectancy of that item when compared with other products of a similar type. On the other hand, when one discusses the quality of shrimp or beef, durability and life span are not considerations. Shrimp is considered better quality when it is larger and fresher. Beef is considered better quality when it is lean and fresh. In architecture, the term "quality" again addresses different issues; here, the term may apply to design, the actual building process, or use of different techniques, as well as the physical structure of the building and the building materials used.

In order to get a clear idea about the different types of goods, they could be categorized as follows:

investment industrial goods, such as heavy machines, tractors, and cranes; and

consumptive goods, which really are of two sorts. First there are consumptive industrial goods, such as houses, cars, televisions, lawn mowers, and computers. Then there are consumptive agricultural goods, such as meat, produce, fish, grains, and such.

Considering quality from the environmental and economic aspects, there could be different positions toward quality. Using a monetary consideration, the subjective value of the quality of a product could diminish with the higher price of that product, whereas the higher price of a product with substantially higher quality would have environmentally positive effects. The monetary approach is typical of a society used to quantitative growth with little or no regard for quality. However, if industrial goods fulfill the two main characteristics of quality — a longer life span and increased durability — this product will, in the long run, be advantageous in both economic and environmental aspects.

Does a product of superior quality require more energy and raw materials than an inferior one? Many speculate that this would be the case, but the facts would have to be investigated on an individual basis. Nonetheless, there is much evidence that in the long run, production of higher-quality goods would be more cost-effective and environmentally friendly.

It is clear that finding a unified definition for quality is very difficult. Some people may see quality in more detail, better design, and finishing, items that would justify an increased cost. However, from the standpoint of environmentally safe prosperity, only those products with a longer life span, increased durability, and modular design would fulfill the qualifications of quality. This makes it imperative that design engineers and corporate managers responsible for new product designs consider and integrate at least these three requirements into their new designs. Any added features would simply enhance the marketability of the product and give it a competitive edge over similar items.

PRODUCTIVITY

As Paul Krugman says in his book *The Age of Diminished Expectations*, "productivity isn't everything, but in the long run it is almost everything." Like quality, productivity is difficult to define because of the various beliefs people hold. Although, in principle, there is no dispute regarding the significance of productivity as a key measure of economic vitality and well-being, the differences begin with the conventional definition of productivity and the goals behind it.

As described earlier, productivity simply measures the output per hour of all workers, from regular staff to unpaid family members. It shows how much companies can produce and at what cost. The productivity measure, according to the conventional definition, provides information about quantitative changes.

The two main shortcomings regarding this definition and the way productivity is calculated are that it neglects the qualitative aspect of productivity and does not take into consideration those changes in the area of goods. Additionally, it ignores the productivity issue in the service sector.

It may seem surprising that economic theory has failed to deliver any approach regarding the definition and calculation of productivity in the service sector, much less determine a method for measuring the qualitative aspects of the goods and services. Some attempts, such as that made by P. Ranganath Noyak, a senior vice president at Arthur D. Little, Inc., indicate that to increase the productivity of the white-collar worker requires that one first find out whether they are working on the right projects, how much unnecessary innovation is being undertaken, and how the employees spend their time.

An increase in productivity of goods from a qualitative aspect requires production of more of those items, featuring the principles of environomics, in a given time or producing the same number of items in a shorter time. This would appear to be, in essence, the same definition of increased productivity that is applied in quantitative growth, but in this instance the products follow the principles of environomics. However, when one looks more closely at the issue, the difference is significant.

The reason for the difference is that because productivity is a key barometer for the economic well-being of a nation, an increase in productivity of goods within the specifications of quantitative growth can be environmentally destructive and indirectly inflict damages on the economic well-being of the nation. Measuring productivity of the goods that exhibit features provided by environomics gives a true picture of the economic well-being of a nation. It is imperative that this way of measuring productivity become increasingly popular.

On the one side, a post-material society that is ruled by the principles of environomics will be more service oriented. On the other side, realization of increased quality of life requires an increase in social services, health care, and education. It therefore becomes immensely important that productivity in the service sectors of the economy be improved as well. As an example, one of the main reasons for the suffering in the health care industry — worldwide and in the United States particularly — is the lack of productivity in that sector, exacerbated by greed, monopoly, fraud, and unfair advantage being taken of suffering patients.

The primary reasons for poor productivity in the health care industry are that the structure is fundamentally wrong, the performance of work is time consuming and inefficient, and, rather than complimenting each other, different areas of the field are counterproductive. It should come as no surprise that the health care industry in the United States finds itself in such poor shape at this point in time. If this industry were run like most other businesses, it would have to become more efficient or face bankruptcy.

Quantifying the specifications for measuring productivity in the service-oriented sector is difficult, due to the diversity of services and the intangible nature of the "product." However, guidelines can be developed that could be used to increase the quality, as well as the productivity, in these critical sectors. A comprehensive analysis of this subject is featured in the health care chapter and will not be repeated here.

One of the main considerations in increasing productivity in the service sector involves the ability to perform simultaneously two or more services, instead of only one service per given time and/or cost unit. The higher the variety of services at a constant cost level, combined with a constant time and labor input, the higher the productivity in the service sector. Enterprises providing service must become increasingly multi-functional in nature, capable of providing at least two or more types of service without major interruption or cost increase. In addition, services must be provided in such a manner that there is no unnecessary repetition. Further, results of previous services should be easily accessible to anyone providing subsequent services that require that information.

In plain English, the sum of all services must be achieved in less time and at a lower cost than occurs when the services are performed individually. Although not all aspects of this approach can be applied to all service-providing industries, this strategy provides an excellent guideline for the health care industry. How could this result in environmentally safe prosperity? In a post-material society, the more services you get for the same amount of money or in a shorter period of time or both, the more would be contributed to a higher quality of life.

PROSPERITY-INDUCING TECHNOLOGY

Technology and technological progress, as we know them, bring us the best and the worst of two worlds. Conventional technology provides increased income and an improved standard of living. In short, it contributes to economic growth by increasing productivity in the conventional sense. On the other side of the coin, technology and technological progress destroy the working place and result in a loss of jobs. They lead to enhanced exploitation of raw materials and fossil energy on the one side and the destruction of the environment on the other side. The faster and larger the scale of development and the employment of technology and technological progress, the faster and more encompassing the exploitation and destruction.

Nobody would say that these reasons make technology or technological progress particularly good or bad, because lack of technology would put us back to the level of developing countries. However, it is causing us to confront severe economic and ecological problems. Technology and technical progress have different effects, depending on where and how they are used. Regardless of the level and manner of employment in economy and industry, these effects can be noted without exception, varying only in degree.

Many scientists attempt to distinguish between good and bad technology, recommending that we enhance the use of soft or benign technological approaches and phase out the malignant technology. Again, this simple qualification of technology is not sufficient to provide the best possible results for an environmentally safe prosperity. Additional refinement is required.

The question generally asked is, what is the most desirable technology? This is the wrong question, resulting in erroneous answers. The correct question is, what characteristics should a technology have to contribute to a better quality of life? In other words, what features have to be considered to fulfill the requirements of being environmentally safe and at the same time prosperity-inducing?

There are five main characteristics of a PIT: it must be environmentally safe; it must be designed in such a manner that it can operate on renewable energy sources; it must be based on modular design that allows for changes; it must be decentralized and have the possibility of being available to all or must be centralized for use by the masses; it must be durable and have a long life span.

Although it is understood that incorporating all five features may not always be possible, due to the nature of the technology or the product, the attempt to do so should be the driving force behind any design.

There are two disadvantages to employing PIT. First, when implemented on a large scale, these technologies could jeopardize certain existing businesses, resulting in tremendous financial losses in the business world. Second, they reduce the possibilities for corporate heads to charge the consumer for such items as energy, repairs, and replacement products, thus creating a threat to those who hold the majority of the wealth.

These disadvantages affect a relatively small number of the population. The application of PIT is in the best interest of the general population and provides the only way to improve our quality of life, which includes not only the environmental and economic aspects but also intangibles such as leisure, education, and health care, those conditions necessary for realization of an ideal lifestyle.

In spite of the fact that there is a great deal of potential for opposition from those referred to as the "big boys" in both government and corporate politics, environmental and economic pressures will eventually force the adoption and implementation of PIT. Sooner or later, it will become clear that the big boys are approaching extinction through their own destructive activities. The question remains, when will this occur?

Sharp critics may arise, perceiving a lack of sensitivity or vision for technological progress in the concept of environomics, particularly in the recommendation to switch from quantitative to qualitative growth, as described in this work. There may be some that fear that when the life span and durability of a product are increased, the product may become obsolete during its lifetime. There will be others who perceive quality products as resulting in unemployment of the people who currently produce in quantity or provide replacements.

The next chapter explores these issues and provides examples of how the concepts of environomics can be applied in everyday life.

6

Environomics:
Answers and Examples

One of the major areas of questions seems to be the issue of qualitative growth. One concern is that if we strive for quality, rather than quantity, the price of a product is going to be higher. Although this will probably be the case because of the extra expense of producing a better product, the higher price will be offset by the fact that it will need to be paid less frequently over the same period of time, as shown in the example of the better-quality automobile.

There is a further benefit to the issue of quality. In an economy based on environomics, the manufacturer would be obliged to provide a product that would not break during the warranty period. The warranty would be required for a minimum number of years, covering all parts and labor for that product during the entire length of the warranty. Following the concept of environomics, the manufacturer would have to compete not only in areas of price and features but also in the area of warranty protection, which would serve as documentation of the quality of the product.

The advantage here is that unlike what occurs in our current economy, money for repairs would not be a necessary expenditure. Today, whatever money you spend for repairs (on a car, for instance) is taken away from your disposable income, reducing the amount of money you have available for other purposes.

Some feel that implementation of quality through warranty performance, with minimum requirements on various items, would require some type of governmental intervention, which they feel is against the spirit of a market-oriented economy. In reality, the market-oriented economy already has instances of government intervention to protect the consumer, for example, constraints on air fares and the telephone industry, in the interest of preventing monopolies. Why not enforce a minimum warranty performance on industrial products, increasing it gradually until it meets the principles of environomics? We may find that legislation is unnecessary, that economic and environmental pressure may be sufficient.

This all sounds very well and good, but environmentalists may ask how such concepts will prevent people from destroying our forests and wildlife. How will this concept prevent people from cutting the trees or eradicating our ocean resources? With the current increases in population and the desperate need for residential, industrial, and commercial progress, how will this affect the simple struggle to survive?

Once people understand the benefits of the concept of environomics and begin implementing it, we will begin to see a reversal of the destructive processes in our production methods and an increasing contribution to general prosperity. Some of the environmental problems — destroying of forests, killing of wildlife, and such — must be partially resolved by government bans of these activities and punishment of the violators. However, before this can occur, the people who rely on these sources for survival must be provided opportunities to support themselves and their families with other sources of income.

Population growth is a major concern of many economists and environmentalists alike. We must understand that such growth is often tied directly to a population's standard of living. Until we can create a better social, economic, and health care system, people will continue having large families, viewing the numerous children as a kind of social security for their old age. This is one of the primary reasons for the overpopulation of developing Third World countries.

One of the suggested approaches is population containment. Let us say that a couple is allowed to have two children. With two children, they would receive tax incentives in various areas, assuming that a certain level of economic well-being had been attained for the entire population. If they decide to have more than two children, they would not only lose the initial tax benefits they had been receiving, they would be taxed in some manner for the additional children. This is not to say that people cannot have more than two children; it simply says that additional children will have a financial effect on the entire family, not unlike it does today. However, one cannot tax people if they have nothing with which to pay the tax. Therefore, it is imperative to improve the standard of living of all people in order to make such a policy practical and effective. This is where the concept of environomics is used to boost the general prosperity of all people, not just certain groups.

The world population, currently approximately 5 billion, is increasing by at least 80 million every year, and 90 percent of that growth is occurring in the developing nations, countries where the people are struggling to eke out a bare existence. If we want to survive on this planet, we must prevent these people from continuing in their destructive processes of struggling for survival. The only way we can truly assist these developing nations is to improve their economic, social, and health conditions — their overall standard of living. The tool to doing this is production, done according to the concept of environomics.

Another concern raised by those considering higher quality and longer life spans in relation to manufactured products revolves around developing technology. What good does it do to have a high-quality product if it is obsolete? One of the requirements of prosperity-inducing technology (PIT) is modular design, which allows the replacement of obsolete parts with new ones that incorporate the improved technology without requiring replacement of the entire item. There is a new method of production, called "design for disassembly," that is an initial step in this direction. This methodology, which was applied in the manufacturing of BMW's Roadster model, calls for designing car parts that are easy to snap apart, sort, and recycle. Special elastic joints connect the plastic body components to a zinc-plated, unibody chassis. Doors, side sills, and panels are made of thermoplastic, parts can be fastened or released by a "pop-in-pop-out" process, and old parts are recycled. Development of true modularity in every aspect of a product is an integral part of environomics, especially in regard to the updating of technology.

Some economists have difficulty understanding how environomics will create full employment. If fewer products are needed because of longer life spans, they contend that a number of jobs will be lost. Although this may appear to be an obvious result of the increased quality of goods, the fact is that there would be the potential for more employment and lack of a sufficient labor force.

Due to the limited life span and low durability of the products we currently buy, we are forced to spend part of our future income on repair and replacement of broken parts or replacement of the entire item. This requires that we work additional hours in order to have money for the replacement and repair requirements we have come to expect. If there was no need to provide those monies, one of two things would happen: either the individual would be able to work fewer hours, or the individual could work the same number of hours and have disposable income for additional items. If a product presents all the features of the environomic concept — a longer life span, increased durability, the PIT features, and modular design — the product will never need to be replaced, partially or totally, within its lifetime. The only consideration might be modular updating if new technology was introduced.

As a result of this fact, the owner would now have to work only once for the product, rather than working several times in order to buy several of the same item. The individual may now choose to work the same number of hours and spend the "saved" money on other items, creating an increased demand for these goods, or may elect to reduce the number of hours worked. Sooner or later, the need for material goods would reach a saturation point, and people would tend to work less hours. As a result of the decrease in working hours, more jobs would be free for other workers, assuming the production level remains approximately the same due to an increase in population. New products and technologies would continue to be developed, creating demand and new jobs to fulfill that demand. In addition, global demand for quality United States goods would more than replace any decline in demand resulting from the extended useful life of quality goods, particularly if we have pursued our goal of improving the economic standing of the poorer countries.

If full employment already existed at the time and the population had no desire or need to work longer hours, the problem of an insufficient labor force would occur, necessitating the recruitment of workers from other areas or countries where sufficient labor was available and unemployed. That possibility raises another question. Some feel that if the work was exported to other countries, there might be problems with loss of control, in regard to corporate policies or technology, for instance. In reality, most heads of state would be delighted to have to deal with a full employment problem that required importing foreign labor or exporting work to be done. Bear in mind that the exporting of jobs to other countries, those with sufficient labor forces, would help those countries elevate their standard of living. This fact would be of interest to environmentalists, as the exporting of jobs to these areas would assist developing countries in bringing their people out of the vicious circle of poverty. Eliminating their desperate and destructive struggles for survival by channeling those energies toward productive work and an improved life would aid in protecting the environment and realizing improved economic levels and quality of life for emerging countries.

How would this exporting of jobs and importing of goods affect our trade balance? It must be remembered that we would export jobs only when our labor market had reached a saturation level and we did not have sufficient labor to produce the products we needed. In addition, foreign investments, in the form of transferring jobs to other countries, would bring capital gains. One should realize that an economy developed in accordance with the concept of environomics would pass through different stages of prosperity throughout the world. It would start with agrarian, moving first to industrial, then to service and information, and finally to leisure and intellectual and technical pursuits.

Once an economy has reached its final stage and the people are forced to export industrial jobs to other, less-developed economies, the people of the developed countries would be able to enjoy more leisure or become increasingly active in intellectual matters, depending on their preference. More time spent in intellectual pursuits would ultimately lead to more research and development and additional technical progress. These would benefit the economy as a whole, in the form of either new and improved products or new technology. In addition, there would be capital gains from foreign investments, as a result of having these new products produced in other countries.

The matter of full employment leads many to raise the issue of inflation, a subject to which many countries are extremely sensitive. Environomics does not provide room for inflation, as to the Keynesian and monetarist concepts. In environomics, inflation would not exist, or if it did, it would be negligible due to the trade-off that would take place between working hours and leisure time or intellectual pursuits. Because of this, the economy of that society would progress.

In the monetarist concept, money plays a major role, and the availability of too much money compared with the availability of goods causes the inflationary process to start. The Keynesian approach is different; they see the source of inflation as increased cost, which triggers the wage-price spiral, for instance.

In environomics, price increases would certainly exist, but as a reflection of the integration of improved technological features or the production of a product superior to its predecessor, a true increase in the value of a higher-priced product. Superior quality, modular technology, and, especially, PIT, as well as the other measures of environomics regarding health care and financing options, have a dampening effect on inflation, as we will discuss later in this book. As a result, any nation sensitive to the issue of inflation should have no concerns about implementing the concept of environomics. In fact, those concerned about inflation should be among the first to embrace the concept, because inflation can be curbed by adopting more of the PITs and producing products with a longer life span and increased durability through the use of modular design.

How would one describe an economic boom in an economy based on environomics? In a conventional economy, an economic boom occurs when the economy has been enduring a recession. In an economy based on the environomic concept, which consists of general prosperity and economic well-being, an economic boom makes no sense, because there would have been no prior recession. Economic booms and recessions are phenomenons resulting from the implementation of conventional economic concepts, which have no place in the concept we are encouraging here. However, a boom of sorts could be created in environomics as a result of a breakthrough in technology or as technological progress is made through the use of PITs.

One of the concerns of the politicians and their constituents alike is the manner in which environomics will address the Social Security issue. Environomics provides for dealing with the requirements of older individuals by resolving many of the financial concerns during their younger years. If we produce items with a longer life span — items that will not require replacement — and people purchase these items during their younger years, when they are working the most hours and making the most money, their primary concerns in later years will be for food and clothing and leisure pursuits. The Social Security System would probably continue to exist; however, the participants would be required to contribute substantially less to the fund, as their requirements in their later years would be reduced. The concerns about the high cost of contributing to the fund, the lack of security based on insufficient performance, and the decline in the number of working people would be eliminated, as would the need for increased payments (to counteract inflation, for instance).

In view of the features and practices of environomics, it would appear that energy conservation would not weigh too heavily, assuming that the energy-generating devices are based on PITs that are free and do not pollute the environment. This would be true if we devote our efforts to developing energy-generating concepts based on PIT. In the proposed society, there will be additional time for leisure activity and other pursuits, many of which will require transportation to attend. The primary limitation would be the cost of energy.

Some individuals question whether the implementation of environomics would result in the disintegration of all power plants. This could happen unless the power plants were converted to technology based on the PIT concept and energy could be supplied to customers at a very low price. Regardless of this, the recommendation would be to move to decentralized modular energy systems based on the PIT theory.

Even if we move immediately to the technologies encouraged by environomics, there is a great deal of cleanup work to be done if we are to address the problems we have already caused within our environment and our economy. It is critical that we begin to change our attitudes and approaches immediately if we are to achieve well-being in both areas.

One of the major concerns of the industrial groups is their feeling that environmentalists and their followers are becoming fanatical and powerful. They feel that certain organizations and movements encourage people to reject economically sensible ways of dealing with the environmental problems and, further, promote answers that have already failed the test of time, sometimes at great cost to the human race. The more extreme of these environmental opponents contend that those who pursue such utopian ideas may well turn out to be a greater danger to their fellow citizens than the supposed pollution is, not unlike the way Marxism spread poverty in the name of eliminating it.

There is no question that certain extreme solutions could be counterproductive, but there is no need for this. The reasons for the failure of Marxism and other approaches have been widely discussed and demonstrated, and part of the reason for their failure is because they operate exactly opposite the concept of environomics. If you have followed the fundamentals of environomics objectively, you have noticed there is no element of extremism, nor is a radical approach included. We have not suggested you throw away your car and ride a bicycle everywhere you go; instead, the concept shows how to make a better car by using technologies that are prosperity inducing and environmentally safe.

There should be no conflict of interest between environmental and economic goals if things are done the way they are outlined, in accordance with environomics. The reason there is no sensible way of dealing with the environmental problems in an unregulated, capitalistic economic system is that these problems are cost factors — they reduce the profits of the entrepreneur. The shorter the time an entrepreneur allows to maximize profits, the fewer the incentives and motivations to deal with the environmental problems.

As much as one may agree to the failure of Marxism, it would be wrong and unfair to say that Marxism has contributed to the poverty of the masses in those countries that have followed its dictates. In fact, one could point out that the Marxist philosophy has contributed to the conscience of the working people, encouraging them to strive for material improvements while making the proletariat see such a necessity.

Could environomics lead us to utopia? Why have we not gotten there before now?

Many great thinkers throughout history have proposed schemes for the ideal society. Sir Thomas More, an English statesman, wrote that the ideal society was a commonwealth, governed entirely by reason and free of crime, poverty, injustice, and similar ills. He described such a society in 1516, calling it "utopia," from the Greek word for "nowhere." Today the term "utopian" refers to an imaginary ideal state — idealistic, but not practical, according to Webster's. Karl Marx proposed a utopia where everyone's economic needs were provided for. Neither these, nor any other utopian visions, became reality. The problem was not with the concepts, but with the approaches.

In order to realize a dream, you must have a concept that is right and the will, ability, and desire to work toward accomplishing that dream. These prerequisites did not exist in the past. The British Empire concentrated instead on an exploitive colonial policy. Karl Marx emphasized distribution rather than production, ignoring the fact that without production there is nothing to distribute. These two approaches lacked sound and practical guidelines. Environomics provides such guidelines.

Organized religion preaches that the humanly devised utopia cannot succeed because it does not solve the problems of human nature. Organized religion contends that religion must correct the problems of a secular, consumer-oriented society to reach utopia. Although there is no doubt that spirituality is essential, there is a great deal of wisdom in the concept of "First the body, then the soul," as taught by Zarathustra, the prophet of the Zoroastrians, back in 1080 B.C.

Much has been said and written about "quality of life." What is quality of life from the perspective of environomics? It is impractical to quantify quality of life, knowing that what improves or reduces quality of life differs from one person to the next. However, most would agree that the creation of a sound and safe ecology combined with general prosperity would provide a good foundation for defining quality of life. With these goals achieved, the possibility to improve quality of life in areas such as health care, education, work, leisure, social environment, personal security, and justice exists.

The goal of environomics, as stated previously, is to help realize environmentally safe prosperity. There is a large economic gap between the industrialized nations of the West and the countries of the Third World. The application of the concept of environomics is meant to curb, if not eliminate, the environmentally destructive activities of the people in these Third World countries, where such actions are currently considered necessary in the interest of day-to-day survival. Until we realize economic well-being for the Third World, there is little hope of resolving the environmental problems effectively. All of these factors — economic well-being, changes in philosophy in the areas of manufacturing, new approaches to technology — must be achieved if we are to remove the current threat to mankind and the planet.

7

The Strategy for
Abundant Safe Energy

Finding solutions to the energy problem is so easy, yet so complicated, and so close, yet unreachable. On one side of the coin, it is political suicide not to protect the interests of big business; on the other side of the coin is the lack of a method for making an easy transition from a profitable but environmentally unsafe venture to an environmentally sound one. Few are interested in risking the loss of a fortune for an unforeseen number of years.

There are two awkward points in the current situation. The nations that consume the most energy are those with relatively limited reserves or with the lack of capability to satisfy their needs from domestic sources. Either there is a lack of decision regarding solution of the energy problems or, if a plan exists, it is either condemned to failure or causes long-term devastation to the environment and, eventually, humanity.

Tables 7.1 and 7.2 list some statistics and naked facts that provide us with a better picture of what we are up against.

Two facts can be easily recognized from Tables 7.1 and 7.2. First, the United States consumes more energy than it produces. In 1986, U.S. consumption was 73.9 quadrillion British thermal units (BTUs) and production was only 64.3 quadrillion BTUs. Second, although there is a balance between the production and the consumption of all other sources of energy, a major gap exists in crude oil. The United States produced 18.4 quadrillion BTUs and consumed 31.9 quadrillion BTUs, creating a deficit of 13.5 quadrillion BTUs, which had to be imported.

If one takes a closer look at the energy situation of the major industrialized nations of the West, one finds more or less the same dependency on crude oil, much of which must be imported. Only Norway and Great Britain are self-sufficient, thanks to their domestic resources.

Table 7.3 presents a world summary of production, consumption, and reserves of crude oil, showing the increasing dependency of the oil-

TABLE 7.1

Energy Production by Major Source in the United States
        (1960–1986 in quadrillion British thermal units [BTU])

Major Source	1960	1970	1980	1984	1985	1986
Crude oil	14.9	20.4	18.2	18.9	19.0	18.4
Natural gas liquids	1.5	2.5	2.3	2.3	2.2	2.2
Natural gas	12.7	21.7	19.9	17.9	16.9	16.5
Coal	10.8	14.6	18.6	19.7	19.3	19.5
Nuclear power	Z	0.2	2.7	3.6	4.2	4.5
Hydropower	1.6	2.6	2.9	3.1	2.9	3.0
Others	Z	Z	0.1	0.2	0.2	0.2
Total production	41.5	62.1	64.8	65.8	64.8	64.3

Z = Less than 50 trillion

Source: U.S. Department of Commerce, Bureau of the Census, *Statistical Abstract
of the United States, 1988*, 108th Edition (Washington, D.C., Govermnemt Printing
Office, 1989), p. 535.

TABLE 7.2

Energy Consumption by Major Source in the United States
        (1960–1986 in quadrillion British thermal units [BTU])

Major Source	1960	1970	1980	1984	1985	1986
Crude oil	19.9	29.5	34.2	31.1	30.9	31.9
Natural gas	12.4	21.8	20.4	18.5	17.9	16.5
Coal	9.8	12.3	15.4	17.1	17.5	16.5
Nuclear power	Z	0.2	2.7	3.6	4.2	4.5
Hydropower	1.7	2.7	3.1	3.7	3.4	3.5
Others	Z	Z	0.1	0.2	0.2	0.2
Total consumption	43.8	66.4	76.0	75.1	74.0	73.9

Z = Less than 50 trillion

Source: U.S. Department of Commerce, Bureau of the Census, *Statistical Abstract
of the United States, 1988*, 108th Edition (Washington, D.C., Govermnemt Printing
Office, 1989), p. 535.

consuming nations on the oil-exporting nations. The intention is not
necessarily to demonstrate the political dependency of the importing
nations on the exporting nations but to show that crude oil resources are
limited.

TABLE 7.3

World Summary of Crude Oil Production, Consumption, and Reserves
(1985–1989 in million tons)

	1985	1986	1987	1988	1989
World Oil Production	2,762	2,917	2,910	3,029	3,112
United States	491	477	461	454	427
West Europe	187	194	197	196	191
OPEC	819	957	928	1,032	1,150
World Oil Consumption	2,842	2,925	2,980	3,044	3,064
United States	723	753	768	798	798
West Europe	542	562	563	572	572
Japan	207	214	209	220	231
OPEC	174	177	175	177	179
World Oil Reserves	95,486	95,102	120,466	134,483	136,080
United States	3,770	3,306	3,406	3,572	3,486
West Europe	3,565	2,927	2,928	2,455	2,478
OPEC	64,630	64,937	91,055	103,041	104,217

OPEC = Organization of Petroleum Exporting Countries

Sources: Mineraloelwirtschaftsverband, Mineraloelzahlen, 1989 (Hamburg: ACO Druck GmbH, 1990); and *Oeldorado 87* (Hamburg: ESSO, 1988); *Oeldorado 88* (Hamburg: ESSO, 1989); *Oeldorado 89* (Hamburg: ESSO, 1990).

The political problems concerning the supply of crude oil pale when compared with the limited oil reserves and the environmental damage caused by its continued consumption. Political disagreements and differences can be settled, if not through diplomatic efforts, then through a military showdown, as was demonstrated during the Persian Gulf crisis in 1990 and 1991.

However, should the present level of consumption of crude oil continue, with no increase in use, the presently known crude oil reserves will be exhausted in roughly 40 years. Any increase in the rate of consumption will, of course, hasten the depletion of reserves. The theory of exponential growth applied to consumption of crude oil quickly illustrates the result of increased use.

Table 7.3 illustrates the frightening fact that Japan, a country most anxious for economic growth, has practically no oil reserves and cannot produce oil for its own consumption. However, its great appetite for the world's supply of crude oil in view of its struggle for economic growth could mean even more rapid depletion of the world's oil reserves.

Unfortunately, other industrial nations have an equally healthy appetite, and there seems to be no hesitation in the consumption of the currently identified crude oil reserves.

The statistical data regarding crude oil show its dominant role as the primary source of energy for the Western industrialized nations. Its importance as the main source of raw material for industry cannot be overlooked.

In spite of their significance in industry, as well as in private household use, crude oil and, more precisely, the mineral products are not environmentally friendly; the effects on our ecology are devastating, and the use of mineral products can severely damage and pollute the environment. Their use pollutes air, water, and land, as well as the atmosphere, and does so at a magnitude not reached by any other industrial product. Petroleum products cause pollution not only as primary and secondary sources of energy but also as raw materials derived from the petroleum products.

These facts regarding crude oil should not be interpreted to mean that this source of energy and raw materials is worthless and totally damaging. Used under strict control, petroleum products could have thousands of uses in chemical and pharmaceutical industries, for instance. However, because of the limited oil reserves and the threat of depletion in the near future combined with the damaging effect on the environment, the question remains, what can we substitute for oil as a source of energy? Of course, an effective substitution for crude oil through alternate energy sources would automatically lead to the substitution of other polluting energy sources, such as coal and nuclear energy, as the development progresses.

To be more precise, how can we replace crude oil with environmentally friendly, alternate energy sources? To find an answer to this question, it is necessary to consider what kinds of alternate energy sources exist, what their potential is for replacing crude oil, and their effects on the ecology.

A total substitution for crude oil is advisable already from a political standpoint, as it would contribute to the Western world's independence from the politically unstable oil-exporting nations of the Organization of Petroleum Exporting Countries (OPEC) and the Middle East. The imperative nature of the environmental consideration may be an even stronger incentive, as this concerns the health of the people and the planet, as well as obligations to future generations.

In order to achieve political independence from crude oil, it is necessary to replace crude oil quantitatively as well as qualitatively. As mentioned already, crude oil is not only a primary and secondary source of energy, it is also the main source of raw material for industry. There are very few products on the market today that do not include some kind of crude oil derivative. This means that a total substitution for crude oil requires a source that can provide the features of crude oil as a source of energy *and* as a raw material; otherwise, only partial substitution can take place. Although this requires both qualitative and quantitative substitution, from an ecological standpoint, a partial substitution would be sufficient, particularly if we were to replace crude oil as the primary and secondary energy source, substituting an environmentally friendly and safe source.

The distinction between primary and secondary energy is important in that a secondary energy may be environmentally friendly while its primary source is very damaging and harmful to the ecology; electricity is an excellent example of this. Electricity is an environmentally safe source of energy. If, however, it is produced through nuclear power plants, its primary source — a nuclear power plant using uranium — is extremely damaging to the ecology because of radioactivity and nuclear waste. Conversely, if the electricity is produced through solar power plants, the primary source — the sun — is environmentally safe. In addition, we need to understand that a secondary source is not always ecologically safe, either. Gasoline, a secondary energy source for powering cars, does as much damage to the environment as does crude oil when used to power the plants for generating electricity. As a result, a natural source of energy could have differing effects on the environment as a primary and secondary energy source, depending on how that natural source is used to generate the secondary energy.

This same consideration applies to the secondary energy source, which may depend upon applied technology. Nuclear power is a good example of this. Uranium, as a natural source of primary energy, causes no environmental problems. When used in a nuclear power plant, the secondary energy — electricity — is safe, but the nuclear waste created is detrimental to the environment.

Table 7.4 shows that the only primary energy sources that have no adverse effects on the environment are sun, wind, and water. The other sources are ecologically intolerable and must be avoided, with the exception of natural gas, which could still be accepted to some extent. In addition to the environmental limits, there are other reasons why the future is bleak and serious consideration must be given to alternative energy sources, including the lack of technological and economic feasibility, limited reserves, extremely high development costs, and the

TABLE 7.4

Global Comparison of Ecological Problems Caused by Primary Energy Sources

Primary Energy Source	Different Pollutants and Burdens						Quantity/ Cost
	Air	Water	Noise	Waste	Heat	Visual	
Oil	Large	Large	Large	Little	High	Large	Medium
Coal	Large	Little	Medium	Large	Medium	Large	Large
Tar sand	Large	Large	Large	Large	High	Large	Large
Shale oil	Large	Large	Large	Large	High	Large	Large
Waste/garbage	Large	Little	Large	Medium	Medium	Large	Large
Uranium	Large	Large	None	Little	High	Large	Medium
Geothermal	Large	Large	None	None	None	Large	None
Natural gas	Medium	None	None	None	None	Medium	None
Sun	None	None	None	None	None	None	Large
Wind	None	None	None	None	None	None	Large
Water	None	None	None	None	None	None	Medium

Source: Compiled by author.

time factor regarding their large-scale operation. To find the real potential of all alternative energy resources, each of them is analyzed from a critical viewpoint in Table 7.4.

The alternate energy sources that could best substitute for crude oil, in qualitative as well as quantitative aspects, are synthetic oil and gas, the primary sources of which are coal, shale oil, tar sand, and garbage. Whereas coal and shale oil are found in the form of stone, tar sands look like dark brown sand. The structure of garbage depends primarily on the lifestyle of the humans who create it.

Although the research of winning synthetic oil and gas from coal dates back to World War II, and the history of research is much longer than that regarding shale oil and tar sands, the results have not been at all satisfactory, in spite of the fact that coal yields three to four times more synthetic oil than do shale oil and tar sands. The main advantage of synthetic oil and gas is that its effect on air pollution is minimal, and almost negligible, due to its very low sulfur content. This advantage is, however, offset by a series of problems, which have so far prevented its further development.

During the oil crisis of the 1970s, coal was considered as the primary source of energy for the future, at least as a transitional solution until large-scale operations of nuclear or solar energy could be developed. The fact that coal could provide raw materials for the chemical industry made it a promising source. In addition, there was the prospect of being able to win protein from coal.

There were two reasons for the positive potential of coal. First, it existed everywhere in large quantities, and second, it had almost the same specifications as crude oil. However, these advantages were offset by a number of serious problems.

The first issue was the necessity for further development of required technology for producing synthetic oil and gas from coal. Not only did the process require improvement of the technology for removal of the sulfur from coal and for dealing with the necessary gasification and liquefaction of the mineral, but also technology had to deal with the fact that there are different kinds of coal, such as anthracite and brown coal, that have different qualities and specifications.

Seven to eight years are required from the time of exploration to the time a plant is in full operation. Usually, it is more practical and less expensive to develop a new plant than to reopen an old mine.

The labor factor is one of the major obstacles. To keep pace with the new demand for labor, new coal miners would need to be mobilized, and few people have any desire to work in the coal mines. The potential for automation is limited because of the lack of profitability of the operation.

Finally, there are severe environmental problems associated with the use of coal — devastation of the land, removal of the ashes, and potential air pollution from sulfur dioxide.

In addition to these problems, there are other difficulties, specific to each country with coal reserves. In the United States, for instance, there is a lack of transportation facilities, such as railways, rivers, and roads, to accommodate the transport of coal from mines and from production plants to the point of use.

Because of these and other problems, the future of coal as a primary source for producing synthetic oil and gas seems to be limited, if not impossible. Part of the problem is the fact that synthetic oil and gas cannot compete in price with crude oil, and there would be an enormous investment required to attempt the transition. Rising environmental concerns seem to indicate that coal will not even be used in electric generation plants that may be developed in the future.

The world reserves of shale oil are at least several times as large as the crude oil reserves. Considering the 27 countries where shale oil has been found in very large quantities, the United States' reserves are the largest, representing 60 percent of the world shale oil reserves. This is the equivalent of 85 billion tons of crude oil, which corresponds with 63 percent of the total world crude oil reserves, based on proven reserves of

1989. Based on crude oil consumption in 1989, the total shale oil reserves in the United States would provide the equivalent of world oil consumption for approximately 23 years. By comparison, the total crude oil reserves in the United States would last little more than a year to cover the world consumption. Almost 30 percent of these huge U.S. reserves are located in Colorado, Utah, and Wyoming.

In spite of these mammoth reserves in the United States, and the contention that shale oil could provide a remedy to the United States' critical energy situation, there are three groups of problems that must be resolved.

First, we must find the technological solutions to mining and exploitation, distilling, and refining of the shale oil rocks. Problems regarding the exploitation of shale oil occur during the mining process, as unimaginable quantities of shale oil rock must be moved. To extract any significant amount of oil from shale oil rocks, one must remove and process quantities equivalent to the amount of soil dug out of the Panama Canal, and this must occur on a daily basis. Every ton of shale oil rock yields two gallons of oil.

The primary problem in the distilling process is creating and keeping a temperature of 600 degrees Centigrade in order to be able to extract the oil from the rock. Adjusting the refinery to different types of shale oil presents another major problem in this area, adding another burden that prevents this industry from taking off and being used on a large scale.

The second group of problems results from the environmental aspects of developing shale oil. Air and water pollution are caused by the sulfur, benzine, and nitrogen, which also devastate nature in the form of remaining ashes.

The third problem is that of inexpensively procuring sufficient water for the purposes of hydrogenation and the cooling of the synthetic oil extracted from the rocks. This is a major consideration in the shale oil-rich states of Colorado, Utah, and Wyoming, where even the Colorado River cannot provide sufficient water. There are potential sources of water from the Mississippi, but the difficulties of long distance and differing heights must be dealt with. Procurement of water from these sources would demand enormous investment.

In view of these facts, it becomes obvious that a large-scale utilization of shale oil as a major source of energy or as a substitute for crude oil is neither possible nor advisable. In addition, the possibility of severe environmental problems makes this a nonacceptable solution.

The potential reserves of tar sand located on the American continents are even larger than the shale oil, as shown in Table 7.5.

TABLE 7.5
Synthetic Oil from Tar Sand Located in the American Continents
(in billion tons)

Columbia	62
Venezuela	37
Canada	30
United States	1
Total	130

Source: Compiled by author.

The quantity of synthetic oil that could be extracted from tar sand is larger than the total proven crude oil reserves of the world as of 1989. If all other tar sand reserves were known and included in the statistics, the reserves would be further increased, although the identified sources are more than sufficient for the world's needs.

The utilization of tar sand involves the same types of problems we have identified in the use of shale oil, but technology for tar sand is far behind. The high demand for water does not cause as much of a problem in Canada, where the tar sand fields of Athabasca are located next to the Athabasca River in the province of Alberta. This is the site of more than 83 percent of Canada's total tar sand reserves. In the United States, however, there is, again, insufficient water available for the site in Utah.

Like shale oil, tar sand has a low oil content, an average of 12 percent of any extractable quantity of tar sand. As a result, there is little doubt that the United States' tar sand reserves would not provide any potential as a substitute for crude oil, nor could they play any major role as an alternate energy source for the future. This is also true for shale oil.

Coal still plays a significant role as a primary source of energy, but its contribution as a primary source of synthetic oil is doubtful, as is the use of shale oil and tar sand. However, if the world economy continues to be dependent on crude oil until the reserves are exhausted, there will probably be no environment or an economy left to worry about. If timely attempts are undertaken to develop and implement alternate energy sources, these three sources, along with nuclear energy, are the least favorable.

With economic and technical progress, the quantity of garbage produced has increased accordingly, becoming a serious problem for the environment. Recycling of wastes is considered one solution. Garbage consists of organic and inorganic substances, the inorganic materials capable of being recycled and used again. However, a solution is needed for the organic materials. The possibility of converting them into synthetic oil and gas is an attractive alternative.

Pilot plants have been built in several cities, including St. Louis, Baltimore, and San Diego, but so far there has been little success in getting rid of wastes in a harmless manner or extracting enough synthetic oil to make the effort worthwhile. Although we generate twice as much organic waste as inorganic, more than half of the organic material consists of water, limiting the potential for winning synthetic oil and gas economically. Also, organic wastes occur in relatively small quantities and require excessive effort and cost to collect.

For each 1 billion tons of inorganic waste, there are 2 billion tons of organic wastes. Theoretically, this could provide approximately 900 million tons of dry wastes ready for making synthetic oil and gas. If this were the case, that 900 million tons would yield 175 million tons of synthetic oil, which would cover roughly 22 percent of the U.S. oil consumption in 1989. In reality, the useful quantity of waste that would be realized is approximately 136 million tons, which would yield 27 million tons of synthetic oil, about 3.33 percent of 1989 oil consumption in the United States.

There are three methods used to extract synthetic oil and gas from wastes — hydrogenation, pryolyse, and bioconversion. Although bioconversion is a much simpler process than the other two, there has been little development in that area. Approximately 40 percent of the original waste quantity must be burned, creating an ecological problem in the form of air pollution. In spite of a waste growth rate of 5 percent to 8 percent in the industrialized nations of the West, the basic question remains: how does one easily and inexpensively access sufficient quantities of organic wastes to make the effort worthwhile from an economic standpoint?

Environmentally, there is little difference in the use of wastes for synthetic oil and gas. One way or another, removal of garbage must be dealt with. Sooner or later, we will run out of landfill space, and another solution will be required.

The cleanest fossil energy source is natural gas, in spite of the fact that some air pollution is caused through burning. Qualitatively, it can substitute for crude oil quite adequately. In order to make use of this potential energy source, a series of technical, financial, and political problems must be resolved, addressing the nature of natural gas and its distribution throughout the world.

To get a clear idea of the potential of natural gas as a substitute for crude oil, it is necessary to explore that potential from the standpoint of reserves and production, as shown in Tables 7.6 and 7.7. Table 7.6 shows that the world's natural gas reserves have increased based on the latest data available.

The former Soviet Union has the highest natural gas reserve, followed by Iran, the United Arab Emirates (5,683), Saudi Arabia (5,132), the United States, and Qatar (4,616). It is interesting to note that the world natural gas reserves have almost doubled, from 57,910 billion cubic meters in 1973 to 112,947 billion cubic meters in 1989. Although the main increase in these reserves took place primarily in the former Soviet Union, Iran, and Venezuela, the natural gas reserves of the United States began to shrink during this period, from 7,080 billion cubic meters to 4,670 billion.

It is also interesting to note that those countries who have the majority of the reserves — with the exception of the former Soviet Union, the

TABLE 7.6

Development of Natural Gas in the World

(in billions of cubic meters)

	1973	1986	1987	1988	1989
Eastern Bloc Countries	21,080	45,185	42,700	44,177	44,241
Soviet Union (former)	20,000	43,890	41,000	42,450	42,450
Middle East	11,700	26,190	30,705	33,457	34,721
Iran	7,650	12,740	13,850	13,992	14,150
Africa	5,310	5,695	7,040	7,085	7,550
Algeria	3,000	3,000	3,000	2,949	3,226
North America	8,500	8,070	8,060	7,989	7,339
United States	7,080	5,250	5,285	5,298	4,670
Middle and South America	2,590	5,380	6,420	6,684	6,614
Venezuela	1,190	1,670	2,690	2,893	6,614
Western Europe	5,410	1,670	2,690	2,893	6,614
Norway	650	2,820	3,000	2,420	2,325
Indonesia	NA	1,400	2,065	2,366	2,463
Rest of the world	3,320	5,680	6,430	6,872	7,081
World total	57,910	102,735	107,500	111,820	112,947

Sources: Oeldorado 73 (Hamburg: ESSO, 1974); *Oeldorado 86* (Hamburg: ESSO, 1987); *Oeldorado 87* (Hamburg: ESSO, 1988); *Oeldorado 88* (Hamburg: ESSO, 1989); *Oeldorado 89* (Hamburg: ESSO, 1990).

United States, Canada, the Netherlands, Great Britain, and Algeria — make very limited use of this energy source and have not developed its potential.

Japan's situation in regard to natural gas reserves is not any better than its situation with crude oil, the country having only about 30 billion cubic meters in reserves. This is part of the reason why their consumption of natural gas is very limited, roughly 2.1 billion cubic meters.

Table 7.7 presents a complete picture of natural gas production in the world, highlighting the countries with the highest production. In most cases, natural gas cannot be exported or is exported in only small quantities. For this reason, the amount of production generally equals the amount of consumption.

The two countries with the highest production, the former Soviet Union and the United States, present two different aspects. The production capacity of the United States started to drop around 1975 and, since 1985, shows a consistent diminishing trend. The former Soviet Union shows a consistent increase in production for the same time period, accounting for half of the 51 billion cubic meters increase in 1989. Almost 40 percent of the world's natural gas production comes from the former Soviet Union.

TABLE 7.7
World Natural Gas Production
(in billion cubic meters)

	1973	1986	1987	1988	1989
Eastern Bloc Countries	353	506	730	846	873
Soviet Union (former)	289	435	643	770	796
North America	638	617	548	571	576
United States	569	547	464	473	472
Western Europe	168	199	192	185	192
The Netherlands	91	96	81	67	72
Middle East	37	46	64	95	101
Saudi Arabia	3	11	19	29	31
Africa	14	21	50	62	62
Algeria	7	12	37	45	45
Rest of the world	26	60	99	120	122
World total	1,285	1,516	1,758	1,961	2,012

Sources: *Oeldorado 89* (Hamburg: ESSO, 1990).

Table 7.7 also shows that countries in the Middle East (such as Iran) and countries with huge reserves in other parts of the world are the same countries with very low production. Their natural gas industry is only minimally developed, in some instances virtually untapped.

Why is this alternate energy source, much more environmentally friendly than crude oil and coal, being left unused? Like other alternate energy sources, natural gas suffers from technical problems caused primarily by the nature of gas and its geographic distribution. The major problem that plagues the further development of the natural gas industry and prevents consumption in the Western industrialized countries is that exploration of new gas reserves is tremendously expensive. To locate sources in the United States, wells often have to be drilled as deep as 4,600 meters. More than 80 percent of the time, failure is the result.

Importation of natural gas from other countries has some practical limitations. Supertankers must be built with cooling temperatures of minus 160 degrees Centigrade in order to convert the product to liquid gas and transport it over a long distance. Once at its destination, the process would have to be reversed, converting the liquid gas to normal gas.

Although there are immense technical and economic handicaps to be overcome, natural gas could play a dominant role in curbing the increasing global demands for crude oil and energy. In addition, using this energy source would limit or reduce the environmental damage currently being caused by fossil and nuclear energy sources.

To achieve this goal, technical and economic assistance must be provided to those countries that are rich in natural gas reserves. At the very least, they should be encouraged to develop their economies based primarily on gas. This would, to some extent, relieve the environmental burden and ease the transition to an era of environmentally friendly energy sources and technologies.

Natural gas is the most appropriate energy source for a transition period. The success of this energy source depends more on political than on technical or economic decisions. If, for example, political decisions favored economic and technical assistance for such nations as the former Soviet Union or Iran, these countries could begin moving their economies more and more to natural gas. Compensation for this assistance could be made in crude oil, which would serve all involved countries economically. Environmentally, the results would be positive as well, as these countries would reduce the ecologically damaging practices involved with use of crude oil. This type of approach should be considered for all countries with large natural gas reserves.

Sun, water, heat inside the earth's crust (geothermal energy), wind, and uranium are considered as primary energy sources. These could partially substitute for crude oil quantitatively in areas where crude oil and its derivatives are used to generate energy and power, the utilization being dependent on the type of technologies employed.

The main contributions of these sources of alternate energy would include generating electricity and powering transportation equipment and factory operations. The major obstacles are not restricted to technology and investment requirements but include the social and economic costs of the transition from one source to the other. Further handicaps occur because of the lack of capability to transfer electric energy over long distances. This aspect has a particular effect on solar energy.

Although the regenerating energy sources — sun, water, earth heat, and wind — are considered environmentally friendly, either they lack well-developed technologies or their large-scale employment is not economically feasible. One of the biggest handicaps to using these alternate energy sources is political, as they are not favored by politicians any more than by leaders of industry. Governments are not yet in a position to provide the huge amounts of money that will be needed to allow industrialists to justify the transition.

It is interesting that uranium and nuclear energy, which lose any advantage when compared with the above energy sources and which also lack sufficiently developed technology to be economically employed, found support from politicians and industry leaders alike. Current technology is not only underdeveloped, it lacks environmentally safe and friendly characteristics. Following is an analysis of these regenerating energy sources and their potential as an alternate to crude oil.

The energy from the sun is the oldest and, by far, the largest and cleanest energy source available to mankind. In fact, all fossil energy sources are the result of a long process caused through sunshine. Even the other alternate energy sources, such as wind and geothermal and tidal power, are created through sunshine. Not only is the sun the source of life on the planet earth, it is also the origin of all alternate energy resources.

Why, then, has this energy never been utilized on a large scale in industry? Millions of solar water heaters are warming homes in Japan, South America, Australia, Israel, and the United States. Solar energy has been used for desalination of sea water in many countries. The fact that the sun can provide an enormous quantity of energy can be documented by a number of examples of its use.

The amount of sunshine that hits the earth during a single day is sufficient to cover the energy demands of humanity for 25 years. The quantity of heat from the sun shining on Lake Erie in Michigan in one day is equivalent to the total annual energy consumption of the United States. The extent of solar energy shining on the roof of a normal house is approximately two to ten times the amount of energy required to heat and cool that house. Finally, based on the hydrogen reserves of the sun, solar energy would last approximately 10 billion years.

In spite of our current modest use of solar energy, its potential is extremely varied. It could be used to heat, cool, and generate electricity, as well as in desalination of sea water and in winning hydrogen to be used as energy.

As yet, the utilization of solar energy has been limited to the building of prototype plants and some initial testing. There are a number of reasons for this. A major reason has been the sources of cheap fossil energy. Then, in the 1960s, hope was centered on nuclear energy. It was only after crude oil and nuclear energy became sources of trouble, both environmentally and politically, that solar energy became attractive. However, due to a series of political and economic factors, the planners in government decided to stick to their old habits, dependency on crude oil continued to grow, and interest in the nuclear energy potential was revived.

The major setback for the solar industry in the United States occurred when the Reagan administration allowed the solar tax credit to expire because of pressure for balancing the budget and dealing with the deficit. The budding U.S. solar industry was killed before it ever got off the ground. Under the Bush administration, we saw no change in attitude, and solar energy would seem to have no future at this point. Admittedly, there are a number of technical handicaps that need to be overcome, but the same is true of nuclear energy, which is receiving a more positive reaction.

Regardless of these factors, solar energy utilization was attempted through various methods, including solar cooking equipment, water heating systems, and desalination plants. There were plans for solar houses and solar farms, a satellite solar power system, and solar sea power plants. Some of the solar energy systems consisted of simple, almost primitive, methods, as evidenced by the solar water heating systems. This was based on a water tank, a solar collector, a pump, and some other fittings and fixtures. The collector was simply copper tubes framed in an insulated, glassed, aluminum box. The system could operate exclusively on solar energy if a small photovoltaic solar panel was added to run the pump, and the simple operation was more productive than the highly sophisticated nuclear power plants.

In an independent study, Amory Lovins' Rocky Mountain Institute concluded that the U.S. government had spent no less than $46 billion to subsidize the nation's energy industry in fiscal 1984. Describing the expenditures in "bang-for-the-buck" terms to a House of Representatives subcommittee, research assistant Richard Heede said that nuclear power, which received almost $16 billion, supplied less than 100,000 BTUs per dollar of subsidy. Comparably calculated, renewable energy sources provided several million BTUs per subsidized dollar. An overwhelming part of this latter performance was the result of the primitive solar water heating system.

More sophisticated and high-tech solar system designs, as seen on the Solar Farm, are in the prototype stage in a few of the Southern states in the United States. They are being tested with mixed results. Projects like the Satellite Solar Power System and the Solar Sea Power Plant seem more like science fiction than reality, but they do show what can be done if the financial resources and political support are available.

The main problem with these technologies is not so much the technical challenge as the lack of knowledge about their long-term environmental effect on the earth and its inhabitants. For example, the Satellite Solar Power System requires placing two huge solar power plants, each with 25 square kilometers of surface area covered with photovoltaic solar cells, into orbit a distance of 36,000 kilometers away from the earth. The Satellite Solar Power System, capable of providing 5000 megawatts, would collect electricity from the sun, convert it to microwaves, and beam them to the station on earth, where they would be converted back to electricity for consumption. The major problems connected with projects of this magnitude are generally the tremendous financial and technological requirements. In the case of the Satellite Solar Power System, the specific problem is the lack of knowledge about the long-term effects of microwaves on humans and the environment. Similar types of problems with different emphasis can be found in other highly sophisticated solar systems.

There is no question that we have a long way to go before solar energy can be implemented effectively on a large scale. However, one of the major issues is the fact that people believe harnessing solar energy must take place with sophisticated and extraordinary technologies, technologies that have yet to be developed. The following suggestions indicate how untrue this is and recommend steps that can be taken immediately to begin use of this energy source.

An immediate goal should be the installation of solar water heating systems in every house in the United States where there is sufficient solar energy to run the system at least four months out of the year. To implement this measure, a no-interest financing plan could be offered to provide the money necessary for homeowners to complete the installation. After a grace period of five years, homeowners who do not have installed solar water heating systems would be taxed. The penalty tax should be low, starting with perhaps 0.5 percent of the home's assessed value, then escalating gradually until a solar system is installed. The possibility of tax penalties, combined with the financial incentive of easy financing and tax avoidance, would encourage homeowners to use the alternate energy source.

One advantage of this plan compared with the tax credit approach of the 1980s is that it does not involve a large initial fiscal burden, nor does it allow for the type of manipulation that was one of the biggest drawbacks of the earlier incentives. Implementation of this approach would revive the currently starving solar industry and begin progress in research and development.

There are further advantages. First, there would be relatively little initial cost associated with the practice: the homeowners would be compensated for their investment by the savings derived through use of solar energy as opposed to purchased energy; there would be little, if any, cost to government; there are no political implications, and the measure is not politically unpopular. Best of all, solar energy utilization would be implemented in an environmentally safe way that contributes to the general prosperity. A prosperity-inducing technology (PIT) type of technology would have made strides toward the future. Imagine the long-term results if this plan were to be implemented by other nations.

Although the technology that provides solar water heating capabilities is simple and primitive, it works and has reached a high level of development. As the related technological development progresses, there is little chance that this method will become obsolete. The system is economically feasible, as the flat plate solar collector is inexpensive to manufacture and is all that is needed in areas with a lot of sunshine. In other areas where fewer of the sun's rays reach the earth, evacuated high-temperature solar collectors, using a vacuum for insulation, could be employed with satisfactory results. The next step, in all areas, would be the use of solar energy to run space heaters.

The second phase would be for the government to encourage inventors and entrepreneurs in the further development of the solar system, which I will refer to here as a decentralized modular solar system (DMSS). The existing water heating solar systems could be integrated in DMSS (with some modification), and the DMSS not only would be able to generate heat for water, homes, spas, and swimming pools but also would provide for cooling, through thermal heat collected from solar energy. Although there is a great deal of necessary research and development to be done, this technology is the easiest and least expensive to develop and implement on a large scale.

The third stage would be the further development and integration of photovoltaic solar cells in DMSS to provide for generating and supplying electricity for the electrical appliances and devices throughout the home. Insulating the home and using more efficient electrical equipment would result in a drastic reduction in the amount of energy required. During the construction of new homes and facilities, many features of passive solar heating and cooling should be simultaneously employed, resulting in a lower demand on the DMSS, which would reduce the investment cost.

One consideration would be the development of a modernized passive solar air-conditioning system, similar to the wind grapper of ancient times that was described at the beginning of this book. This system would work particularly well in warm areas with little or no humidity.

The development and completion of the DMSS is not particularly complicated, nor is it unrealistic. At most, it requires a mid-tech capability with plenty of political backing to smooth the path for the economic considerations for research and development. Over the long run, the cost of that development will be considerably reduced when viewed on a per piece basis.

The next step would be to develop a much larger type of DMSS, one that could be used in a power plant to supply energy to commercial and industrial buildings with insufficient space for an independent source of energy. To relieve the burdens caused by environmentally damaging power plants, the possibilities and potential of systems such as the Solar Farm and the Solar Sea Power Plant should be further explored, bearing in mind that there could be reduced need for these plants if every nation were to adapt the solar energy systems described above. With this approach, there would be limited need or justification for the Satellite Solar Power System.

One of the keys to large-scale utilization of solar energy is an economic and political climate that allows the exploration of possibilities to answer the many questions currently surrounding the issue. How does one make use of the DMSS possible in every climate? Perhaps through development of a chemical that reacts to outside temperature, the temperature raising as outside temperatures drop and lowering as outside temperatures rise. If this could be accomplished, the already-developed solar collectors that feature double channels and heat exchangers could be used to provide energy year round, day and night, requiring little, if any, storage capacity.

Is such a thing possible? I think it is, although I do not claim that the way I have described DMSS provides a valid, working technology. The critical issues are that we begin thinking in terms of possibilities and that a climate is created that encourages new inventions, drastic improvements, and development of existing technology. I was fortunate in having almost a decade of intense involvement in the solar industry, working with design and development as well as manufacturing and marketing. That experience is the basis of my belief that DMSS can be easily developed and implemented, because many of the components of the system are already in existence.

Water is another clean source of energy that can be used to generate electricity through hydroelectric power plants. Water can also be used to win hydrogen as a source of fuel and energy for homes, industry, and transportation. Compared with electricity, hydrogen is a tertiary source of energy, because electricity is required to produce hydrogen. In addition to hydroelectric power plants, there are other methods of generating electricity from water, such as tidal power and fusion, several of which we will discuss here.

Probably the cleanest source of electricity is the hydroelectric power plant, which is also an almost inexhaustible source. In spite of the fact hydroelectric power usage in Scandinavian countries is more than 13 percent and in Canada is 7.5 percent, worldwide consumption is only 2 percent. In some countries, such as Switzerland, hydroelectric power has reached its full capacity, while the largest untapped resources for hydroelectric power plants exist in the developing countries. Handicaps to development in these areas are the lack of necessary technology and the ability to transfer electrical energy over a long distance.

Unfortunately, because of these issues, there is little possibility of direct utilization of hydroelectric power, even in the industrialized nations. This is unfortunate, as the only potential environmental damage would result from the construction of the dams that are normally required.

Tidal power plants are another option for harnessing and utilizing water power. These could be located on the natural coasts, the turbines run by the high and low tidal waves to generate electricity. If it were possible to harness and utilize all the tidal power in the world, we could provide half of the world's electrical demands. However, implementation of this option poses two practical problems. The majority of the coastlines lack sufficient and constant tidal waves, the first prerequisite for harnessing the power. Equally important, the financial burden of building such a plant is not justified by the benefits. All things considered, there are only 20 locations where a tidal power plant could be used. If the full potential of these limited locations were utilized, they could provide at most only 2 percent of the electricity generated by hydroelectric power plants.

In consideration of their limited potential in generating electricity, tidal power plants could play no practical role in helping to meet the world's energy demands. There is currently only one tidal power plant in operation, built in 1966 in LaRauce, France.

Even with large-scale use of the various alternate energy sources, such as solar, nuclear, geothermal, and fusion, there would be a definite need for hydrogen. Not all energy demands can be met by electricity. In addition, electricity from these sources can be neither stored nor transferred over longer distances. One example of the limitations of the alternate energy sources is the electric automobile. In spite of various efforts, actual usage is limited, as is true in airplanes. Hydrogen provides a real alternative to electrical power where the limits of the latter become obvious.

The most important feature of hydrogen is its environmentally friendly character. Once burned, it evaporates in the form of steam without causing any kind of pollution. In addition, it exists in unlimited quantity. The biggest disadvantages of hydrogen are the high cost of production and the extremely high possibility of explosion during storage and distribution. However, the solutions to the technical problems are not as difficult as resolving the economic aspects of its production and distribution.

At least four techniques for production of hydrogen from water are generally considered: electrolysis, endothermic chemical decomposition, photolysis, and bioconversion. Only electrolysis has been proven in practice.

Because hydrogen is not a primary energy source and electrical energy is required to produce it as a secondary source, an economic breakthrough in the use of this source is possible only if electricity is available at a reasonable price.

As time passes and scientists become more and more disenchanted with nuclear energy and the possibility of a technological breakthrough in regard to fusion, they are more and more favoring the employment of solar energy to produce hydrogen. This could be made to work by having huge plants consisting of solar photovoltaic panels for generating electricity. The electrical power could then be used to separate hydrogen from water through a process of electrolysis. Later, the produced hydrogen could be used again as fuel to generate electricity in power plants where the capability of transferring electricity does not exist. Hydrogen also could be used to heat homes and commercial facilities or to power automobile and airplane motors.

There is little doubt that hydrogen will be the fuel of the near future. It provides all the features of the PIT concept. Serious attempts at its development as a source of energy must be made very soon.

For the past 40 years, scientists have sought to duplicate the process that fires the sun through nuclear fusion, but after an estimated $20 billion in research, a breakthrough in generating the process is at least decades away. The United States alone has spent almost $6.5 billion since 1951. In 1989, Utah's Stanley Pons and Britain's Martin Fleischmann claimed to have achieved cold fusion in a jar, an announcement that excited the world's scientific community, but the euphoria did not last long; the claim turned out to be overly hasty and with no substance.

Nuclear fusion, as compared with nuclear fission, is considered the proper approach to energy alternatives for two reasons: first, the existence of unlimited fuel to run the fusion reactors, and second, the fact that it is environmentally friendly. Deuterium, the isotope of hydrogen, is the main element of its fuel and exists in unlimited quantity in sea water; its reserves could last for billions of years. The other isotope, tritium, is derived from the light metal lithium. Lithium can be won from sea water as well, which increases the reserves to an unlimited level. Its environmentally friendly character is due to the fact that deuterium is extremely safe as a fuel and causes no dilemma with handling the nuclear wastes, one of the major concerns where nuclear fission is concerned.

Energy experts calculate that the cost of generating electricity through nuclear fusion would be very low compared with other methods. The current cost of fuel compared with the total cost of operation is 40 percent in power plants run on fossil fuels and 20 percent in conventional power plants. The use of nuclear fusion power plants would reduce the cost to 1 percent.

In spite of these positive and encouraging facts, fusion technology is far from a breakthrough. It could be decades before a fusion reaction can be demonstrated in laboratories. Should successful laboratory testing be accomplished, it would probably be two or three decades before we would see a large-scale operation based on nuclear fusion.

As promising as nuclear fusion appears to be, even its long-term prospects for providing a remedy to energy demands are uncertain. Use of this approach in the short-term energy crises is out of the question, as we have shown. It is critical that funding be allocated for its development as a future alternate energy source, but it will be at least 50 years before it will be an available solution to our energy problems.

The cleanest source of energy we could employ would be power from generators hooked up to windmills. Wind energy is an attractive alternative for areas where there is sufficient wind. Its biggest drawback for potential large-scale implementation is the relatively high investment cost, caused mainly by the storage system. As with other alternate energy technologies, windmills must be further developed. Once that is done and usage is more efficient and investment cost reduced, its usefulness can be applied in many areas. The primary role of wind energy would be its use as a complementary source to other alternate energy sources.

Currently, nuclear power plants are fueled only by uranium. Should breeder reactors ever be developed, the possibility of employing thorium and plutonium, highly radioactive elements, can be realized. Converting uranium ore into useful nuclear fuel requires huge mining operations as well as the enrichment of uranium, a complicated industrial process.

Uranium is found in nature in three forms, the isotopes of uranium 243, 235, and 238. Most of the uranium is in uranium 238, which contains only about 0.7 percent of that in uranium 235, the isotope that undergoes fission, releasing heat within the reactor. Because of this, the types of reactors used in the United States require that the fuel be enriched by increasing the concentration of uranium 235. Thus, expansion of nuclear power plants dictates a simultaneous expansion of the uranium-enriching plants; this could be a major obstacle to serious expansion of nuclear fission.

The biggest problem with uranium is that its known reserves are limited, probably much lower than those of any single fossil energy source. In addition, it takes an average of eight years to progress from exploration of a reserve to exploitation of the resources. Unless breeder reactors are developed to replace conventional nuclear reactors very soon, the limited uranium resources place a drastic limit on the usefulness of nuclear power plants. Different technologies and the associated implications would, however, determine the future possibilities for nuclear fission.

After almost half a century of intensive research and development of the utilization of nuclear energy, the results are relatively small. In the United States, where nuclear energy has been most progressive, the total energy production is not as high as that achieved by burning wood. Surprisingly, both politicians and industry leaders tend to continue down a failed road. Taking some of the main aspects of nuclear technology into consideration, it becomes clear that it not only cannot contribute significantly to the solution of the energy problems, it also should not be employed in the first place. The following considerations show why existing power plants should be phased out and deactivated.

Two types of nuclear reactors are commercially available, the light water reactor (LWR) and the high-temperature gas-cooled reactor (HTGR). LWRs may be either pressurized water reactors or boiling water reactors. The LWR uses water both as a coolant, to transport the heat released in fission, and as a moderator, to slow down the fast neutrons produced in fission. The HTGR is cooled by helium and moderated by graphite.

The problems associated with nuclear reactors are multifarious. The potential devastation does not justify continuation of use of this source of energy. Neither type of reactor is technologically well-developed, as documented through their inefficiency of extracting the energy contained in uranium. The reactors utilize only one percent of the existing energy in uranium, wasting the natural reserves and depleting what reserves we have in a short time.

Existing nuclear reactors contain the threat of meltdown, similar to the disasters at Chernobyl or Three Mile Island. Newer designs, such as the ones from Westinghouse or General Atomics of San Diego, promise to resolve the problems with a meltdown and eliminate any other disasters that could present a similar serious threat. However, these designs exist only on paper. Although they may be theoretically sound, no one knows yet whether they will actually work.

As far as the serious environmental problems associated with the use of nuclear reactors, the new designs provide no solutions. The most dangerous problem is the deadly effect of the highly radioactive nuclear wastes, which are being stored like so many nuclear time bombs. They could detonate by accident at any time in the next 10,000 years and wipe out humanity. There is no justification for the irresponsibility that has created such a long-term potential threat. The waste heat and escape of enormous amounts of radioactive emissions from the power plants create further problems for both people and the environment.

Once their usefulness is over, deactivating the nuclear power plants presents another major technological and environmental problem. No one knows how to accomplish the task. Every nuclear power plant in existence becomes a nuclear time bomb.

In consideration of these facts, who would want to have their electricity generated from such a source? One may care very little about a threat in the long-distant future, but the nuclear power plants are a serious threat to you and me and to our children. This fact should generate concern and action on the part of all of us.

In the 1970s, high hopes were set on breeder reactors, anticipating a real breakthrough for the utilization of nuclear fission on a large scale. The breeder reactors were considered to have three advantages over the conventional nuclear reactors: they would have a higher performance in generating electricity by using less fuel, they would have a higher efficiency and could use uranium 238 (which existed in abundance), and they would create less waste heat. It is a blessing, however, that a breeder reactor was never completed to the point of being able to breed, although the Soviets did put a breeder reactor into operation. The potential environmental problems connected with breeder reactors make the problems with conventional reactors pale in comparison.

Breeder reactors use plutonium 239 as fuel. There is no question that plutonium is a valuable fuel — 1 kilogram of plutonium delivers the same amount of energy as 3 million kilograms of coal. However, plutonium is the most dangerous and poisonous material known. In addition, the radioactive half-life of plutonium 239 is 24,000 years. In the event of a major accident, this would quite possibly result in the essentially permanent contamination of an entire area. Given the fact that a breeder reactor would breed four tons of plutonium by an input of three tons, it becomes evident that if breeder reactors were employed on a large scale, the entire world would, theoretically, become contaminated forever.

In retrospect, one can view the failure of the breeder reactors and the limited employment of conventional nuclear reactors as a blessing. Nuclear energy, regardless of the manner in which its use is considered, is clearly a prosperity-decreasing technology (PDT) type of technology, to be avoided totally. The United States and its citizens would be best served if rather than pursuing nuclear energy, they were to abandon it altogether, as quickly as possible.

Having reviewed the potential of alternate energy sources and technologies as well as suggestions regarding the PIT and PDT characteristics of these choices, this analysis would not be complete without recognizing the importance of energy conservation. There is no doubt that the economy must keep on going. However, a great deal can be done by implementing energy conservation, without causing adverse effects, cutting corners, or creating major inconvenience.

The development of automobile engines should encompass technology that would increase the mileage per gallon without drastically affecting the performance of the car. Homes and other buildings could be insulated for more efficient use of energy for heating and cooling purposes, reducing the requirements for that energy. Installing a special type of heat exchanger in existing air-conditioning systems can utilize waste heat to heat water; this action also would make the air-conditioning system run more efficiently. The benefits derived from heat exchangers is two-fold, saving energy to heat water and requiring less energy to run the air-conditioning system. Heat pumps are another example of energy conservation, as they heat water more efficiently.

Many other examples exist, which would exceed the capacity of this book if we were to attempt to explore them here. However, it is imperative to realize that until alternate energy technologies and sources are developed, energy conservation is the most effective way of handling the problems of energy demands. Environmentally, conservation is the safest approach. Much can be done in this area, which has almost unlimited potential, particularly in the Western industrialized nations.

The only magic answer to abundant and safe energy is a combination of energy conservation and the promotion of PIT alternative energy resources. At the same time, PDT energy technologies should be phased out gradually and eventually abandoned altogether. The final chapter in this book provides a vision of the world as it could be if the concepts presented are applied. It is probable that environmental and economic pressures may eventually lead our activities in this direction; it is to be hoped that this will happen before a serious disaster occurs or irreversible measures are implemented.

8

Affordable Universal Health Care

Superficially, the availability or lack of health care would seem to have little relevance to the environment, other than the problems associated with the disposal of medical waste. However, inasmuch as the availability of affordable universal health care is unquestionably relevant to the general prosperity, it has an impact on the environment. A healthy society would be more inclined to maintain a healthy environment. From the standpoint of people, the health of its inhabitants is more important than the health of the planet itself; in fact, the health of its inhabitants is synonymous with the health of the planet. If humans are healthy, there will be a strong desire to maintain the health of the planet on which they live and efforts will be made to assure that life is safe and enjoyable. Conversely, if the inhabitants are sick, lacking in good health, there is little reason for them to care about the health of their planet. When an individual's or a family's existence is in question, the matters of environment and ecology hold little importance.

Protecting the environment is one of the two main goals of environomics; improving the standard of living to a level of general prosperity is the other. An important prerequisite for realization of the latter is that society be healthy, physically and psychologically. The availability of health care is a cornerstone of anyone's definition of quality of life. In this book, health care also serves as an example of the service sector and of how productivity can be improved in the service sector.

To achieve the goal of keeping people healthy, or to at least provide them the necessary means to regain their health to the greatest extent possible, requires a universally effective and productive health care system. Current health care systems lack these features entirely.

The different health care systems can be categorized into two main groups, controlled and uncontrolled. The latter sometimes features some elements of control, as seen in the Medicare and Medicaid programs in the United States, which makes the entire system semiuncontrolled. Controlled health care systems are found in countries with a system of socialized medicine, comparable to those of Canada and most of the European countries. The uncontrolled health care system is best documented in the U.S. health care industry, regardless of some elements of control in Medicare and Medicaid.

The major obstacle inherent in both types of health care systems is the lack of productivity. In spite of the fact that a socialized or controlled health care system makes health care available to practically all people of that society at a relatively lower cost than in an uncontrolled or semi-controlled system, the symptoms and sickness of both systems are almost identical. The only differences are that in a controlled health care system, the costs are better regulated and health care is provided to all people, which are not true in uncontrolled systems.

Both health care systems suffer from four major and chronic problems: lack of productivity, collective monopoly (especially in the uncontrolled system), manipulation and disposition of resources, and areas of defensive medicine.

There is probably no other business sector that has such a lack in productivity as the health care industry. This has occurred because the health care givers, namely, the doctors and hospitals, are in an enviable position that exists in no other profession with the exception of the legal profession. There are two reasons for this. A person suffering from pain and illness cannot be very demanding or choosy and must apply for help from a doctor, just as an individual seeking legal remedy must employ a lawyer. As a result, the legal and medical professions can perform at the speed of a snail and yet charge exorbitant fees. In addition, the entire system is designed in such a way that it leads to a lack of productivity and an explosion of costs. This has little to do with the types of services that a doctor or surgeon may perform, a misconception held by many in both types of health care systems.

Instead of doctors who specialize in different fields joining forces and complementing each other's skills, offering a complete service to their patients and thereby cutting operational costs and preventing waste, they establish clinics. Here, a few doctors who are specialized in the same field operate in a manner that results in low productivity, repeated costs, and waste to the patient and/or the insurance company.

Recall the definition for productivity in the service sector provided earlier in this book. Translated to the health care industry, an increase in productivity is achieved only when the doctor follows medical guidelines or practice procedures that allows the patients to be treated in the shortest period. This can be achieved only if the practice is set up in a manner designed to prevent wasted time, repeated tests, unnecessary procedures, and such. The less time it takes the patient to complete this routine, the less cost would be associated with it, and higher productivity would result.

To increase the quality and cost efficiency of health care, two or more services, instead of one, must be provided simultaneously at the same time and/or cost unit. To achieve this goal, multispecialty clinics need to be established where doctors specializing in different fields of medicine could provide complete treatment to the patient in the least possible time at the lowest cost. This eliminates the need for the patient to run from one doctor to another, paying for repeated tests and procedures that represent a waste of time and money, a problem common to the present health care systems.

The existence of the collective monopoly in the medical profession is an obstacle that requires serious attention if the health care system is to be freed from its own sickness. The reason for using the term "collective" to describe the monopoly condition of the medical professions is that contrary to other monopolies, the collective monopoly here consists of a large number of doctors and hospitals who impose the price they want to charge for their services.

This situation is resolved in the controlled health care system to a satisfactory degree, which is why it costs less than an uncontrolled system like that seen in the United States. In the controlled system, the doctors and hospitals are obligated to charge for their services and performance according to a price schedule provided by the government. In an uncontrolled system, such as in the United States, one cannot necessarily appease anger over high medical bills by going to another doctor or hospital. Because none of them are required to abide by any kind of price schedule (unless they accept Medicaid or Medicare), there is no guarantee that changing doctors or hospitals will result in a reduced charge.

The phenomenons of manipulation and disposition of resources in the medical field results in a wide range of problems common to both controlled and uncontrolled health care systems. The only difference is that in the uncontrolled system, this is stronger and deeper.

In both systems, it is common practice for manipulation of the different arts to take place for the enrichment of the doctors and hospitals. These practices are neither secret nor are they the subject on which this book is concentrating; however, it is safe to say that procedures change as clinics grow from individual ownership to a larger partnership or entity.

In clinics owned by a single individual or a small group of doctors, it is possible for a patient to be treated and have the cost charged to a relative's insurance policy, a practice an honest doctor should avoid. One of the well-known policies is the practice of having frequent and unnecessary tests and procedures done by institutions in which the doctor(s) has direct or indirect interests. There is also the consideration of unnecessary surgeries, estimated to range from 20 to 60 percent, depending upon the procedure. Surgeons do not get paid not to operate.

The uncontrolled health care system suffers further from the problems caused by defensive medicine. Because the lawyers want their share of the profit to be made from the prospering health care industry in the United States, they have developed the practice of filing lawsuits against doctors who commit medical malpractice. This legal practice has created a vicious circle, contributing to ever-increasing insurance premiums for both doctors and patients and to an increased practice of defensive medicine. The American Medical Association estimates that defensive actions, linked to fear of lawsuits, may add $20 billion a year to national spending on medical care. Add $13 billion per year in malpractice awards, and you can see $33 billion wasted unnecessarily. The most distressing feature of these unscrupulous activities is the multiplicational effects of the costs, which continually escalate health care costs. The potential end result is unknown.

Before a solution to the problem of health care is presented, we need to see how this information is reflected in facts and figures in the United States and other countries.

Probably the best and worst of health care can be found in the United States. There is little doubt that the best hospitals and most famous doctors in the world are found here. Medical research and technology in the United States is at the top of the scale, and the doctors in this country routinely perform miracles that others dare not dream of. The down side of this situation is that health care costs the nation the astronomical sum of more than $700 billion annually. At the same time, 34 million of the 250 million residents of the United States lack any kind of health insurance.

Considering the amount of money Americans spend each year on health care, one would think every American would be able to get the Rolls Royce of health care, especially when expenditures are compared with those of other industrialized nations of the world. Health care costs in the United States make up 12 percent of its GNP, as contrasted to 8 percent in Germany, 6.5 percent in Japan, and less than 6 percent in Great Britain. Based on per capita spending for health care, the United

States again beats all other industrialized nations, with an annual per capita cost of $2,350 in 1990. In comparison, Canada's per capita cost was $1,680, Germany was $1,230, Italy was $1,050, and Great Britain, $835. Given this information, it is somewhat perplexing that life expectancy in the United States is lower than in 15 other countries and that the infant mortality rate is higher than that of 23 other countries, placing the United States at somewhat the same level as that of developing nations of the Third World.

It is clear that there is no relation between the extremely high expenditures for health care in the United States and medical success, considering that 34 million Americans lack any kind of health insurance and are exposed to devastating threats to their economic well-being should they experience a severe illness or the necessity of surgery. Those who do have health insurance either are covered insufficiently or are subject to numerous restrictions concerning the use of their insurance. These facts have resulted in restricting the freedom of many U.S. workers in terms of changing jobs or relocating to other areas of the country, particularly if they have a chronic illness. A major consideration in considering a new or different job is the type of insurance coverage the new employer will provide. Only a few, mostly the rich and affluent, can afford to carry adequate private health insurance, and these individuals are the ones who could afford the medical bills if they did not have insurance coverage.

Medicare and Medicaid help to ease the situation to some extent, but with mixed results. At the height of President Johnson's Great Society in 1965, Medicaid and Medicare bills were passed. These two pieces of legislation were to serve similar goals — extending health coverage segments of the population considered to be at risk, Medicaid in the case of the poor and Medicare in the case of the elderly.

Although Medicare has been a success, Medicaid lacked the necessary support, in spite of the explosive program costs. The program began in 1966 with a $1.6 billion budget and grew to a $52 billion program in 1988. The major problem with Medicaid is that in spite of the rising costs, many doctors and clinics are unwilling to accept and treat Medicaid patients. Because the beneficiaries of the program are the poor and the old, they can seldom get help otherwise.

The biggest failure of the Medicaid program is that its explosive cost does not correspond to the growing number of needy people enrolling in it. There are currently 26 million people in the program, only 4 million more than in 1975. Further, the percentage of poor covered by Medicaid has dropped from 63 percent to about 50 percent. Although the Medicare program is successful, it applies only to individuals over the age of 65; at that point, anyone can use Medicare, regardless of their financial needs.

Pressures are mounting to curb the United States health care system and its runaway costs. These pressures are coming not from the 34 million uninsured Americans but from businesses, who see the soaring costs eating into their profits. Health care costs used to be estimated at 4 percent to 6 percent of a company's profit; today, it costs businesses 25 percent to 50 percent to provide health care insurance to their employees.

Efforts to reform the United States health care system can be divided into two groups. The first group prefers some kind of social health care system, similar to the one in Canada, based on a general health insurance that could be regulated by government. This might be similar to the policy in Great Britain or the mixed organization found in Germany, creating a controlled or semicontrolled health care system. Among this group are mostly labor organizations and politicians from the Democratic party. The second group favors avoiding experimentation with other health care systems and maintaining the existing system with a provision to provide general health insurance. The proponents of this group are primarily doctors and other health care providers, who are best served under the existing system.

Regardless of the direction taken, health care systems — whether controlled or uncontrolled — must become as productive and efficient as possible. The problems are not so much systems-related as they are structure-related, having to do with obsolete medical structures and methods of operation. Exorbitant fees for doctors, hospitals, and other institutions must be eliminated, and limits must be placed on exploitive activities.

It is foolish to imagine that if we could just implement socialized medicine, such as those systems in Canada, Germany, or Great Britain, we would be a happy nation with nothing to worry about where health is concerned. If this were the solution, it could be easily accomplished. In reality, socialized medicine suffers from the same problems our own system has: escalating costs and gross inefficiency.

The problems in the U.S. health care system go beyond the tremendous costs and the fact that 34 million Americans are uninsured. Political remedies, such as tax credits or "play or pay" plans aimed at universal coverage, will not solve the health care problem in the United States or anywhere else; they would only perpetuate and expand a hopelessly inefficient and failed system. Although we may blame problems in various industrial sectors on others, the way we blame the Japanese for the ills of the auto industry, the problems of the U.S. health care sector are homemade.

Tax credits to low-income families, financing through government intervention, or financing through tax dollars is not the answer. The primary objective of a policy based on tax incentives should be to promote only those projects that follow government guidelines, guidelines that would result in increasing productivity within the industry. Breaking up the collective monopoly of the health care sector and creating competition through increased productivity and quality medicine is necessary. Health care costs must be reduced through increased productivity, without negatively affecting the quality of care or the incentives of care givers. If the health care clinics and institutions improve their operations in such a manner that they can perform more and better services at the same cost or within the same time, productivity is increased.

We need to define our objectives before we can resolve the problems with the health care system.

- The cost of health care must be reduced, delivery must be efficient, and productivity must be increased, especially from the qualitative standpoint.
- Health care insurance should be affordable and available to all.
- Everybody should receive the highest quality of health care possible.
- Victims of medical malpractice should receive all of the compensation. Although this aspect of health care plays a small role in other countries, it is an important aspect in the United States.

In order to realize the first three objectives, the medical profession must become market oriented and will require an entrepreneurial spirit to guide it. A new system must be created under which performance is consistent, procedures are structured and efficient, facilities are clean and modern, and individual outlets are profitable. None of the existing health care organizations, such as preferred provider organizations or the health maintenance organization (HMO), fit these criteria. Either the quality of service drops with the decreasing cost or the necessary services do not exist. Conversely, any increase in quality or performance is associated with a tremendous increase in costs.

The model that most closely coincides with this new concept is the HMO with staff doctors. Again, the problem is that the staff doctors are general practitioners who function as gatekeepers. They diagnose the malady and then send the patient to the appropriate specialist. At this point, when the patient must see a specialist or, worse yet, several specialists, the process becomes costly and time-consuming, discouraging the patient from seeking further treatment. This factor reduces the quality of health care at the expense of the patient, and there is no positive productivity anywhere in the system.

The ideal situation would be entrepreneurial, multispecialty clinics. Standard operating guidelines would be developed for the doctors practicing in these clinics, as well as a fee schedule for the treatment offered. Member patients would pay a flat monthly fee, similar to health insurance premiums. Doctors would be salaried and would have no ownership in the clinic, thus avoiding a conflict of interest. Profit-sharing incentives would be given to all employees of each clinic. The most positive result of this approach would be the elimination of unnecessary treatment, tests, and surgery; the incentive would be to return the patient to health and complete treatment in the shortest time possible and at the least expense.

An entrepreneurial multispecialty clinic would reduce costs in many ways, through efficiency and economies of scale. Standardized procedures, policies, and accounting would lower costs considerably. The enterprise would be in a strong position for acquiring expensive equipment for its outlets, being able to buy in quantity. In addition, the equipment would be used more effectively and more frequently, reducing the per-patient cost. New discoveries, procedures, and developments could be quickly implemented throughout the network of affiliated clinics.

Most important, the doctors' specialties would compliment each other. (In traditional clinics, costs are driven up by the fact that doctors must derive the maximum income from the limited number of patients they see.) In addition, patients would be able to see different doctors, as required by diagnosis, at the same facility, without traveling around to visit a variety of offices.

What would it cost to set up such an enterprise? The initial cost of a few prototype clinics is estimated at a few million dollars, approximately as much as the present system wastes in 15 minutes. Once operational and profitable, the multispecialty clinics could be franchised across the country. Investors would rush to get involved. As a result, an effective and productive health care system could be created in a very short time without government intervention or significant requirements for capital.

The system would provide quality care at affordable prices and still turn a tidy profit. The clinics would immediately generate significant income simply by accepting Medicare and Medicaid as full payment.

(With appropriate productivity on the part of the providers, current Medicare and Medicaid fee structures would be more than ample.) In the long run, these programs could serve more people at a lower overall price. Preventative medicine would play a major role, not only because this would make sense for the patient, but also because it is simply good business. This is market economy at its best.

The goal is to provide consistent, quality care to everyone in the most efficient manner possible — in short, to make medicine respond to the needs of the market. When productivity in health care is increased, the cost is decreased. This same approach needs to be taken in those countries with other health care systems, including socialized medicine. In order to expand availability and improve the quality of care, the monopoly of the health care sector must be eliminated and replaced with healthy competition.

Once the health care delivery system becomes cost-effective and efficient, the task of providing health care to all Americans becomes relatively easy. "Play or pay," a system that requires employers to either provide coverage for their workers or pay into a pool covering uninsured Americans, would not be an unbearable burden for employers, and tax credits to working people would be meaningful. Medicare and Medicaid costs would be reduced. However, without substantial gains in health care productivity, such programs would only increase unemployment and ultimately bankrupt the nation.

The short-term benefit of reforming the health care industry would be an increase of employment in the industry as new corporations are formed to meet the competitive challenge. The long-term result may well be a reduction in the overall number of health care employees. As this would take place gradually, unemployment would not be a problem, through natural attrition and a change in educational and career goals of the population.

How would the 34 million uninsured Americans benefit from this system? With the cost of health care reduced to manageable proportions, the government could pick up the tab for these people, partly out of the savings in Medicare and Medicaid that would result from reduced medical costs.

The problem of the rights of malpractice victims remains. The new system would go a long way toward eliminating incompetent and incapable doctors, as no entrepreneurial venture would tolerate an employee who cost it money. However, medical malpractice cannot be avoided entirely. Certain measures will, of course, require comprehensive legislation, rather than the piecemeal solutions that are periodically proposed.

The government should create a compensation policy to protect the rights of malpractice victims, rather than to enrich lawyers. Guidelines should be developed by which the severity of damages caused to the victims can be calculated. A panel, consisting of both specialists/experts and normal citizens, would decide the validity of the claim, the damage(s) involved, and the amount of compensation to be paid. This panel should be changed on a regular basis to prevent manipulation of any kind. Regulations to eliminate incompetent or unlicensed doctors from the medical community would greatly reduce malpractice by simple prevention.

Finally, regulation of lawyers' fees, to reduce or eliminate their participation in malpractice settlements, not only would save a few billion dollars for the unfortunate few victims but also would eliminate tens of billions of dollars per year in needless defensive medical procedures and exorbitant malpractice insurance premiums currently carried by the medical profession.

The implementation of this concept would resolve the problems described earlier that plague the health care industry worldwide and would increase productivity and quality. We would have a system that for the first time, would serve the people effectively and comprehensively.

9

Obstacles Facing Environmental Goals

One would think that recognizing environmental problems would lead people, especially those responsible, to resolve them. Unfortunately, this is seldom the case. The reasons are all too familiar.

With few exceptions, politicians and executives are driven primarily by a strong desire for power and money, whether this is viewed and achieved in the political arena or at the corporate business level. Although few political positions pay well enough that one could be enriched on the salary, the position is associated with the type of power that pays off indirectly in the long run, usually due to favors during the period of political tenure. Individuals who have retired from a political career are often found in various lucrative positions in big corporations. Not everyone is as fortunate as Ronald Reagan, who reportedly received $3 million for speaking engagements in Japan, but most politicians find that their positions enable them to considerably enlarge the amount of money in their coffers, often during their term of office.

There exists another driving force — a desire to leave a mark on history. Almost all politicians with great ambitions are driven by this desire. History is full of examples, and recent events document the trend: Ayatollah Khomeini's revolution in Iran, for the spread of Islam in the Middle East; Saddam Hussein's dream of reviving Babylon; President Bush's involvement in the Persian Gulf War, in the interest of defeating aggression. All are evidence of this force.

Politicians with ambitions to power must be devoted to the well-being of the military-industrial complex within their country. A strong military presence poses a psychological, as well as physical, deterrent to others. However, developing and maintaining a strong military structure is extremely difficult and expensive, especially when the need for such power has been reduced. Struggles to develop or maintain a strong military presence can result in ingenious policies and practices requiring great forethought and shrewdness to assure implementation.

When the Iraqis began attempting to develop their military power in the 1970s, they found a serious partner in the Germans. Although many other countries supplied various kinds of weapons and diverse military technology to Iraq, the Germans were guided by two powerful motivations — money and military know-how. Why should they lose business to other countries when they could get it for themselves? In addition, developing and refining military technology at someone else's expense was an opportunity that should not be allowed to pass. Many of the famous and potent German companies were involved in developing weapons of mass destruction for Iraq and Saddam Hussein. The German government closed its eyes and ignored the involvement of the German companies. Not only did the revenues benefit the German economy, but also the blueprints of those weaponry systems would be in the drawers of the German firms, should they ever be needed, all at no cost to the German government. Although the Germans routinely and consistently denied their lack of desire to become a military superpower after the unification of East and West Germany, it would have been shortsighted not to consider the possibility. In reality, the motivation for involvement in developing weapon systems had been present prior to the unification of the two countries and the end of the Cold War.

With the end of the Cold War, the military-industrial complexes of the world began to suffer enormously. There was a very real threat that the industrial base that supported the army would erode to the point that there would be no potential to build the next generation of weapon systems, nor would they be able to satisfy the demand for the existing weapon system. If the army were to ask General Dynamics Corporation to step up production tomorrow, it would be 14 months before new tanks could roll out the door. In order for the military-industrial complex to prosper, or even to maintain its existing potential, some kind of international tension — such as that of the Cold War or periodic smaller wars around the globe — is necessary. With the Cold War at an end and the Persian Gulf War ending without any massive destruction of weapons systems, particularly on the Allied side, adaptation of an emergency plan was necessary. This plan required the building of a new generation of weapons systems, particularly those that would contribute to manufacturers who were most affected from an economic standpoint.

One might assume there is little reason to worry, regardless of the problems facing military-industrial complexes worldwide, as all countries would face the same problems. However, for countries like the United

States who want to maintain their supremacy in weapon technology, it is imperative to continue with the development and manufacture of the new generation weapon systems. This is an attempt not only to keep ahead of other nations but also to prevent erosion of the industrial base altogether. However, it must be recognized that militarism dries out the economy and courts ecological disaster, with tremendous implications to both political and human rights.

It is in the interests of the politicians to keep the military-industrial complex active. Other industries also exercise their influence on politicians, either through their lobbying groups or because they expect a return on their financial investment in the individual's campaign. Many times, laws are passed that are clearly in favor of specific industries, usually as a result of one of these issues. A prime example of this is the lack of legislation for the automobile industry, an absence of the types of regulations and restrictions that are found in other countries and are certainly needed in the United States. The same examples can be found in the insurance, banking, and chemical industries. The average U.S. worker pays little attention to these issues until one gets out of control, as happened with the savings and loan institutions.

The same influences drive the actions of the leaders of industry, often referred to as the "big boys." The right and wrong of their activities are determined by the same interests as the actions of the politicians, tempered only by the type of industry in which they are involved. These individuals are interested in corporate position and money, their decisions dictated by the need to maximize profits for their corporation. This is the basis for many of our economic and environmental problems.

We hear of exciting inventions that would bring enormous benefits to the consumer. Before we see the positive results, a corporate giant in the industry has purchased the patent and decided not to implement the project. In the interest of avoiding billions of dollars of loss to the industry leaders and preventing any threat to the existence of existing giants, the product is simply eliminated from the market. There is little incentive for a company to adapt a new technology, in spite of bright promises for the future of both the industry and the environment, if it means the potential loss of existing revenues, regardless of their impact on the environment. With no financial incentive, the new technology is neglected or ignored. Present profits and the potential for maximizing a current sure thing in the immediate future are much more attractive to corporate executives and stockholders interested only in the bottom line and their dividend checks. It is not so much a lack of foresight or an unwillingness to invest in the future of the environment as it is a question of decreasing profits and jeopardizing of their position.

If an industry does develop a technology or achieve an exciting breakthrough, this may not be immediately implemented and passed on to the consumer. Although there would be an expected transition period as a result of capital requirements and testing and development, there is also the consideration of other industries that are somehow related and dependent upon the current methodology. A car manufacturer would not immediately adapt methods and technologies that would cut the use of gasoline drastically or make it obsolete, recognizing the adverse impact such an action would have on the oil industry. The same type of behavior applies to oil companies. It is an unwritten rule, practiced throughout the industrial complex.

As long as these attitudes exist among the politicians and corporate and industry leaders, the economy and environment will suffer as they now do. A drastic change in attitude and approach is imperative. How to initiate and implement this change is a question not easily answered. It will require a series of projects, proposals, and plans that can be reviewed by an objective and impartial body of decision makers who are capable of reviewing the alternatives and choosing those that are most beneficial to the world population and our environment. There are certain prerequisites if we are to attain an economic system in a new order that will adapt and implement the concept of environomics.

What economic system would be appropriate to accomplish this? Let us consider the shortcomings of the two major economic systems.

After the fall of communism in the former USSR and the other Eastern European countries, the West celebrated the victory of capitalism and the free market economy. In fact, both systems have failed when one considers their inability to resolve the economic and social needs of the people in a satisfactory manner and their devastating effects on the environment. The accomplishments of capitalism and the free market economy, considered superior in regard to the production of material goods, have been achieved at the expense and exploitation of our natural resources. The solution must be searched for in the concept of environomics, which promotes the ecological-social market economy. Otherwise, attempts to find resolution in mere free market economy will result in extending the same failed practices to other parts of the world. The result will be failure in economies and devastation of natural resources and ecological factors in the emerging countries, just as we currently see in industrialized nations of the West.

The events in the former USSR indicate the failure of communism. However, in many ways, the theories of a free market economy have failed as well. The symptoms of this failure are well-known — unemployment, inflation, lack of universal access to health care, hostile industry takeovers, the insecure future of Social Security, energy uncertainty, environmental problems, and so forth.

To create an effective and fair world order, it is necessary to include and fulfill the political, economic, environmental, and social requirements of all peoples and nations. The mere mention of these four areas of concern presents an indication of the scope of the difficulties and tasks to be addressed. However, to gain satisfactory results, it is imperative that a global way of thinking dominate all future decisions and activities based on the concept of environomics. The implementation of these measures must take place under the forces of ecological-social market economy as opposed to free market economy, without letting the word "social" cause any confusion.

There is little doubt that a market economy is the way to go, but some social elements must be included in order to prevent the ills so characteristic of free market economies. This may sound familiar, and you may rightly say that the need for such measures has long been known and some have even been implemented at times. There is a distinguishing difference between the implementation of certain social measures in a conventional manner and the proposal being made here.

In conventional methods, a social measure of any nature was achieved primarily through taxation, more taxes or newer taxes being implemented to finance the social program. That approach represents the true spirit not of a market economy but of a socialized economy. Some countries, like those of the communist world, were totally socialized. In Western Europe, the economies are a combination of socialized and market economies. In the United States, we see primarily free market forces in action, with small socialized segments, such as Medicaid.

The approach advocated here is not to let the spirit of market economy prevail, in the interest of preventing financing through taxation; tax incentives, rather than taxation, should be used. This approach imposes penalties for not following the direction set by policy. Government responsibility should be intervention only in the sense of channeling its policy in the right direction; the rest of the task should be left to the market forces.

The realization of solar energy projects through tax incentives and penalties, as described earlier, demonstrates an example of this approach. The same policy can be applied to health care, with tax incentives offered to entrepreneurs and the market forces doing the rest. This would see the creation of an effective and affordable health care system almost overnight. In addition to implementing the concept of environomics under the ecological-social market economy forces described above, further search must be made to identify the elements that would shape the political, economic, social, and environmental aspects of the new order.

In realization of the new order, the main task of politics would be to bring democracy to all authoritarian countries, liberating the people of those nations from selfish and cruel despots. This can be done only with sincere interest and advice from the United States. Even without the crumbling of the Soviet Union, this burden would have fallen on the shoulders of the Americans.

The biggest problem in this regard is that U.S. policymakers have not yet realized the limitations or the long-term implications of promoting and supporting the power of their puppets in foreign countries. The administration of the United States must learn to direct its policy toward the needs of the people of the involved countries, instead of their rulers. The rule of despots, religious theocrats, kings, sheiks, and other brutal and exploitive rulers must end.

Religious persecution must become a thing of the past. Freedom must be extended to all religions and their believers. It is one of the primary rights of a human to believe and practice a chosen religion. The importance of this matter can be recognized when one realizes that most of the complicated political problems of our current world, as well as our history, have resulted from the intolerance of stronger religious groups for the weaker groups in various countries and regions of the world.

In addition, we must promote international organizations, particularly the United Nations. This organization must take a more pragmatic shape, reflecting the realities of the world's political and economic structure. For instance, Germany and Japan, two major world economic powers, are currently excluded as members of the U.N. Security Council, a truly unrealistic situation. Attempts must be made to make the United Nations an unbiased and effective international organization, serving in the general interest and well-being of all nations.

The main economic problem that must be resolved is the fair distribution and availability of natural resources, including food and technology. The exploitation of one country by another must be eliminated.

Because the prosperity or poverty of billions of people hangs on the health of a few currencies, that is, the dollar, yen, pound sterling, franc, and Deutsche mark, any mismanagement would have international repercussions. Therefore, financially irresponsible countries should be held responsible, and their freedom of movement should be restricted by creation of a new organization that would function as a watchdog and dictate guidelines to be followed.

The implementation of the concept of environomics would prevent environmental problems from occurring, especially in areas of industrial production, and may well reduce the ecologically destructive activities of people in other areas. Nonetheless, in many areas, national and international legislation and regulations will be required to protect the natural resources so crucial for the continued existence of humanity.

The scope of responsibilities and tasks necessary to satisfy the enormous growing social needs of the people of each society is as far-reaching and comprehensive as the first three factors. Although each society has its specific needs and challenges, all societies have concerns regarding education, justice, liberty, freedom, human rights, and leisure.

Undoubtedly, three nations will play major roles and serve as models in shaping the new order: Germany, Japan, and the United States. The democratic political institutions in most of the countries in the world would be patterned after the U.S. manner. The German ecological-social structure — still in the process of development — would be used as a guiding model for other nations. The Japanese would be best equipped to integrate and implement the concept of environomics in the production of industrial goods after that country realizes the economic edge this will give them over other nations.

10

The Key to General Prosperity

As important as it is to provide a clean and pollution-free environment, the establishment of worldwide prosperity is an absolute necessity. That prosperity is dependent on fiscal policies that will improve product distribution among the population.

Product production based on the concept of environomics will certainly help create the pollution-free environment so important to all our futures. However, in order to produce a general prosperity, a prosperity necessary to the maintenance of such an environment, these products must be distributed among the people of this country and, more importantly, the world. That distribution is, like production, accomplished through the use of money.

Money was originally meant to serve simply as a means of accomplishing certain transactions and creating capital or wealth. Its function as a means of transaction resulted from the problems originally associated with barter, a system in which people swapped the goods they had for the goods they needed. The use of money made the transactions for goods and services more convenient by attaching a monetary value to each and assuring that one could procure what one needed. Money's function as capital occurred when people had more money from selling their goods than they required for the purchase of other items. The lack of need for this surplus money led to an accumulation of capital, and that is where the problems started.

Much has been said and many books and articles written about money and capital. These two items have played a significant role in conflicts among individuals and countries alike. It is common knowledge and a well-documented fact that money and capital have been used as usury, as a means to gain power and exploit people.

In order to realize the benefits of environomics, it is important that money and capital be better controlled to eliminate the adverse and often

devastating trend that makes general prosperity impossible, thereby eliminating the potential for a safe ecology.

Certainly, money is going to continue as the usual means of helping to
realize the environomics society. This chapter not only will concentrate
on problems related to money and capital but also will seek a solution that
allows us to use money and capital in a more constructive manner, one
that makes the realization of the concept of environomics possible. In
other words, this chapter should help to determine how money can be put
to proper use in achieving the goals of environomics, including the
creation of a safe and sound ecology and production of products
incorporating features from the concept of environomics.

It is equally important that we make it possible for all people, or at least
an overwhelming majority of the people, to own and benefit from these
products. The general prosperity of a nation can be achieved only when
its people can own these products as easily as possible without throwing
the economy of that nation totally out of kilter.

The best indication of general prosperity is when the vast majority of
the people own such things as a house and a car (or some other means of
transportation) while benefitting from such basic services as good health
care and adequate education. The issue for discussion is how to make
these services and goods available to the general population in such a
manner that people will not be required to spend a major part of their life
and energy working for them.

There is no doubt that it is practically impossible to make these things
available to each and every person. Regardless of the adequacy of economic measures and policies, there will always be people who are home-
less, poor, invalid, sick, or mentally retarded, people who cannot do
things on their own. These people will need the government's help, just
as they do today, and that is why we have government programs to help
care for them.

The concern of environomics is the average individual, the working
people, who endeavor to obtain these goods and services, individuals
who have every right to them.

It should be understood that the realization of general prosperity
does not require that each person has a uniform house or car or any
other product. This would be counterproductive, and very few of us
would have any desire to strive for the realization of such a society.
The concept of environomics calls for a free choice of goods, an availability of a variety of these types of goods, and a society in which
obtaining these goods does not enslave people from monetary and time
standpoints.

Various individuals from the areas of economics, banking, and financing may raise questions regarding the implementation of the environomic concept from their point of interest. This chapter will attempt to answer these questions and concerns.

One of the major issues in the environomics concept of prosperity is that of interest and financing. From the Islamic viewpoint, interest and usury are considered to be the major sources of economic disparity, and they argue that an economy without interest would immediately improve. The Western economists disagree, pointing out that those economies that do not include interest are doing poorly or are in a state of collapse. They point to the Soviet Union, whose economy was based on a form of socialism, the basic principle of which precludes interest. According to Karl Marx, interest is "an unearned income." Some Marxist economists consider interest, as well as profit, to be a form of theft. The only economic system that appears to be doing fairly well today is capitalism, and capitalism is based on the interest rate.

Financiers contend that the interest rate is necessary as a method to manipulate the price of products and the income from them, adding that without a system of credit and interest, people who are not independently wealthy would not be able to buy the goods and services they need. They argue that the result of that would be widespread unemployment because of the extreme decrease in demand for products.

Bankers argue that without the interest rate as an instrument of manipulation, during times of high inflation or unemployment, we would not be able to control the economy, and inflation and unemployment would run rampant.

In reality, the reduction of real interest rates to a minimum is a significant tool for creating general prosperity. High interest rates have virtually bankrupted much of the United States and continue to enslave the working middle class, preventing their attainment of a higher standard of living. In many cases, interest costs result in individuals paying for goods even after the products are no longer functional and, at the same time, driving up replacement costs. Many of our domestic problems would resolve themselves if this trend was reversed.

Those who do not believe in interest propose that interest be replaced with dividends. As an example, a company has two major sources for obtaining financing — through issuing common stocks or through borrowing the money. If the money is borrowed, the company has to pay interest on the amount borrowed, regardless of its earning situation. On the other hand, if the money is obtained through issuing common stock and the company suffers a loss or does not do well financially, it can reduce or eliminate the payment of dividends for that period. In reality, borrowing the money, which requires payment of interest, may threaten the very existence of the company because of the repayment require-ments, while issuing common stock and withholding dividend payments may give it the necessary chance for survival.

Although some may argue that no one would want to invest money in a new company or a company doing poorly, that is not quite accurate. If one had a promising start-up company or an existing firm with promising new technology, money could be obtained through venture capital and the issuing of common stock more easily than if the owners tried to borrow money from a financial institution that would require an excess of collateral.

Some will argue that interest induces saving, acting as an incentive for people to save money, thus promoting a healthy economy; this is called the classical theory of interest rate. However, none of the fundamental points in John Maynard Keynes' book *The General Theory of Employ-ment, Interest and Money* indicated that interest induces saving. People save, regardless of the interest rate. Although Keynes did not talk about zero interest rate, he did say that lowered interest rates achieve a higher degree of economic growth. If we take this theory to the extreme, we could conclude that when there is no interest rate, we achieve the highest rate of growth, all other factors remaining the same.

Based on the Keynesian economic theory, zero interest or low interest rates could induce economic growth but could also create an economy of galloping inflation. This is invalid, according to the concept of environomics.

Paying interest on borrowed money creates higher costs for the purchaser throughout the system. If money is borrowed for purposes of production, the interest that must be paid on that money is added to the cost of the product. Next, the purchaser must pay interest on the money borrowed in order to buy the product. In this instance, a not uncommon occurrence, the buyer is penalized twice by interest payments. Assume that a company borrows money to start its operation or to extend or enhance the production of a certain product. Because it has to pay a certain amount of interest on the borrowed money, this cost factor is added to the price of the product. The consumer is actually paying the interest for the producer. Depending on the need for financing at differ-ent stages of product research and development, this borrowing of money, payment of interest, and passing of cost could repeat itself. Now, if the buyer has to finance the product in order to purchase it, an interest rate, usually substantial, will be charged on that borrowed money.

Because the company's interest is figured into the price and the consumer is paying it at the point of purchase, the buyer is paying interest on interest.

In a society based on environomics, the goal is to make goods available to the largest number of people in the shortest possible time. An economy developed on the concept of environomics would not have the problems associated with existing economic concepts, whether capitalistic or socialistic.

For the proper and successful development of an economy based on the environomics concept, it is of great significance that interest rates be eliminated or kept to a very low rate, a maximum of 2 to 3 percent, for example. The most desirable, and perhaps the optimum, situation would be achieved if the interest rate was totally eliminated.

What would this do to banks? The banking industry does not exist exclusively on the difference between the high interest rates for borrowing and the lower interest rates for saving. They are active in other fields, such as mutual funds, which could provide profits. In addition, banks could charge fees for the maintenance of checking accounts, which would contribute to the income of the bank.

It must be recognized that 14 percent or more of the financial wealth of this country is deposited in commercial banks, where it is earning no interest. These monies could be used to generate income. There are a number of possibilities for the banking industry to become involved in the positive activities of environomics. Although this book does not extend to specific solutions and proposals for individual industries, there is little doubt that the brilliant minds and financial geniuses in the banking industry will discover that making money within the new concept is not difficult.

Financial institutions, if they can contribute to the general prosperity outlined under environomics, will find a place in the future as well; if not, they will need to diversify into other areas. Using General Motors Acceptance Corporation (GMAC) as an example, let us look at a possible future scenario. The parent company, General Motors, wants to sell its products and not to lose the market to competitors. GMAC could offer 0 percent financing for some selected vehicle models and offer other models at a much lower interest rate than available at commercial banks. In some instances, GMAC and others already have rebates for individuals who pay cash for their automobiles. In an economy based on the concept of environomics, there would be more use of zero or low-interest financing.

In spite of current promotions for what is referred to as "giveaway" financing, the finance companies are not losing money. The purchase price of the car is increased or the costs of promotions are calculated into the price of the car before it is offered to customers. The difference is that the price, instead of the interest rate, is manipulated. This is a perfectly acceptable practice; you must be able to manipulate prices in order to sell cars. However, if your prices are too high, you lose your market to your competition. By manipulating the price of the item, rather than the interest rate, companies remain in a positive position for selling. Because the competition would have the same option of manipulating price instead of interest, there would be little change in the competitive arena. The advantage to the consumer would be the elimination of long-term interest costs, which drive the actual price of an automobile to half again the stated purchase price.

Within the concept of environomics, recession, unemployment, and inflation would cease, thus eliminating the need for the Federal Reserve Bank to control the economy to avoid these negative occurrences. Instead, the Bank would simply monitor the volume of money in circulation.

Money and capital would continue to be used. At present, we are using them to maintain quantitative growth, producing products with a short life span and limited durability — in other words, poor quality. This practice is detrimental to both the environment and the economy. The more we strive toward quantitative growth, the more we speed up the destruction of the environment. At the same time, people cannot prosper if they have to continually replace and repair products that are still being paid for, with payments that include large amounts of interest.

The main intention, therefore, is to reverse these trends and use money and capital in a positive way for the realization of the goals set forth in environomics, recognizing that production is what causes wealth, not redistribution.

To fully understand the far-reaching implications of this issue, we need to go back to the topic of growth. Actually, there are three possible growth rates and developments — diminishing, steady, and increasing (Figure 10.1).

Diminishing development occurs when the initial high rate of growth starts to decrease, until it stabilizes at an optimum point. The best example of this type of growth is the growth of the human body. From the point of birth, it continues to grow for 18 or 20 years, at which point it reaches its maximum height. Once this has been achieved, further development of the curve continues, with a tendency to decrease as the person gets older and starts to shrink.

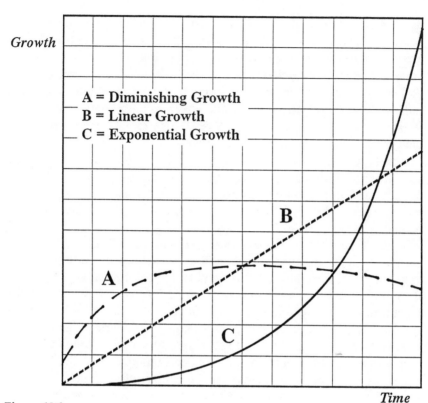

Figure 10.1
Different Types of Growth

Steady growth is also known as linear growth. The development of this type of growth continues periodically, with a constant rate of growth, which finally ends up in unrealistic dimensions.

The third type of growth, exponential growth, is a permanently increasing development in growth with a doubling of rate, a process that doubles its rates in comparison with the previous rate. Exponential growth is extraordinary in nature, and the speed with which it develops is amazing. To understand the tremendous potential of exponential growth, one needs to remember the story regarding the coming into being of the chess game, in which the founder of the game asked the king to double his reward for each additional block of wheat he produced. Using this system, he received a single wheat for the first block, two for the second, four for the third, eight for the fourth, and so on. Initially, the king thought this wish could be satisfied with a few sacks of wheat. Later, he discovered that even if he had collected all the wheat in his country, he could not have satisfied the requirements. When exponential calculations are carried through, one discovers that by doubling the initial single wheat 63 times, one reaches a total of 18.5 trillion wheats, approximately 740 billion tons of wheat. This amount is approximately 440 times today's world production and would cover an entire nation the size of West Germany with a four-meter layer. This example demonstrates the danger and unreality of exponential growth.

This type of growth exists in only two areas of the economy. The first area affected is quantitative growth, and the second is interest. We have already discussed quantitative growth and its devastating impact on the environment, which will become more and more destructive if exponential growth continues in this area.

What do politicians and economists really mean when they talk about a certain annual percentage of economic growth? With only 1 percent annual growth, the initial quantity would double in 72 years; at 2 percent, the initial would increase four times over; at 3 percent, it would increase eight times over. Taken to an annual percentage of 12 percent, we would see more than 4000 times the initial quantity. Considering this, it is easy to see how even 0.1 percent could change results over the long term.

It seems that this factor either has been ignored by politicians and economic planners in the past or the magnitude of the results were not realized when they were planning and exploring percentile growth. In the 1960s and 1970s, a 6 to 7 percent growth in energy was forecasted, and plans were made to expand the nuclear power plants accordingly. Even now, responsible politicians and economists talk about an annual increase in economic growth of 3 to 4 percent, and in some cases, they hope for 6 percent to fight inflation and unemployment. Are they at all aware of the tremendous dimensions and consequences of their demands?

Given a past growth of 2.4 percent annually, over a period of 30 years, we would reach the point where we would produce twice as much as we consume today; at a 4 percent growth rate, we would produce three times as much and, at 6 percent, almost six times more than currently. A limit to exponential growth is becoming more and more critical as time passes.

Had the quantitative growth been accompanied with qualitative growth of the same percentage, the world would have been provided with products of all types that would have been available to almost everyone; general prosperity would have been achieved. Instead, with only quantitative growth, the exploitation of raw materials and fossil energy was accelerated, which led simultaneously to pollution and a gradual destruction of the environment — a real prosperity was never achieved!

In view of the damaging potential of exponential growth, it is necessary to explore whether the same phenomenon exists in regard to money and interest. If it does, what are the possible effects and what is the extent of the potential damage?

If a person deposits a given amount of money in an interest-bearing account with a fixed interest rate and lets the interest income compound as part of the investment, it will grow exponentially. The amount of time it takes to double depends, as we already know, on the rate of interest paid. In other words, the compound interest generates growth with doubling rates, and the period for doubling depends on the rate of interest. This could be calculated by dividing the number 72 by the interest rate, which equals the time required to double the money. The following chart demonstrates the time required to double the money by different interest rates.

Interest rates	3%	4%	6%	9%	12%
Years required to double money	24	18	12	8	6
Years to increase to 128 times	168	126	84	56	42

Now, let us see how this translates into depositing an amount of only $10,000 into an account that bears interest at 9 percent and allowing the interest to remain in the account. After a period of eight years, this amount doubles. The initial amount of $10,000 needs only double itself, through interest and accumulation, seven times to exceed the $1 million mark. In 56 years, the initial investment would have grown to the amount of $1,280,000. To carry the calculation to further reaches, after 136 years, which would allow the amount to double itself 17 times, the initial $10,000 would be worth $1,310,720,000.

This illustration brings out two points. First, we are all aware that money neither grows on trees nor breeds like a rabbit. A lot of people have to work in order for a relative few to have the money to put into the interest-bearing accounts and allow the amount to accumulate and build. If the number of people living on investment exceeded the number of working people, the entire system would fall apart.

Second, each currency is eventually condemned to self-destruction through the effects of compound interest. In the end, even the individuals holding the vast amounts of capital would lose. In basic English, if the majority of the working people, who carry the burden for a relatively small number of people who benefit from the interest and the compound interest, continue growing poorer and poorer as the other group gets richer and richer, the system will fail entirely at some point in time.

How high is the actual burden of interest and compound interest on the economy? To get a realistic picture, one needs to add up all the interest charges reflected in the retail prices of goods and services. This approach would be very expensive and practically impossible, even if each enterprise would make such information available.

The total interest income of an individual household is calculated by adding up all savings and multiplying that number by an average interest rate. The same procedure could be employed to calculate the total interest burden of the economy, using the sum of all invested capital and multiplying by the average interest rate. The ratio between interest and capital — the amount of capital simply eaten away by interest — is a matter of great concern and indicates the need for drastic change.

To see where this leads, one needs to take the GNP of an economy and divide it by the total amount of interest burden that year. Usually, the relationship between these two factors is one to four! One quarter of the GNP flows into the pockets of the banks, money managers, and other holders of capital. Every fourth dollar goes toward an interest payment without any actual activity or visible service being performed, resulting in money breeding artificially.

As these illustrations and explanations demonstrate, serious thought must be paid to the destructive and damaging effects of interest as regards the environment and prosperity. In order to implement the other principles of environomics successfully and make the concept as a whole succeed, it is imperative that we at least reduce the interest rate to a very low level, ultimately eliminating it entirely.

There are a number of questions to be raised and answered and myriad issues to be explored regarding exactly how to proceed with the implementation of this step, because the entire economy of the Western world is based on interest. However, those questions can be answered, and there are realistic solutions to the problems associated with interest. Dealing with this issue is a major factor in achieving an environmentally safe prosperity.

11

The Mandatory Path: Rational Behavior and Prevention of Waste

---

If our only major task was restoring the environment, if we did not have to be concerned about the world's economy, it would be a blessing. Unfortunately, the economy — worldwide — is in as much of a shambles as the environment, and its future is very bleak if the solution sought to counter the malaise is quantitative economic growth. Developments since the late 1980s show that we cannot continue the past errors and trends in the political-economic areas without risking a devastating future.

The prerequisite for the survival of mankind and the planet is the adoption of rational behavior and prevention of waste. These attitudes are necessary for the implementation of the concepts of environomics, which will allow us to realize environmentally safe prosperity. In this chapter, we will present a cross section of a few current events to demonstrate the necessity of rational behavior and waste prevention.

Two words are often used in connection with political dissidents — "refuge" and "asylum." However, over recent years, these two words have become applicable to a much larger group of individuals as a result of world events. The downfall of the shah of Iran in 1979 led to the subsequent rise of fundamentalist Islam in the Middle East, through Khomeini's radical theocratic regime. The collapse of communism in the Eastern European countries followed. Then we had the two Persian Gulf Wars — the one between Iran and Iraq and the one between Iraq and the Allied Forces. These events have contributed to the worsening economic situation, especially in the developing nations, and as a result, there has been a flood of economic refugees entering the Western industrialized countries. This influx has caused tremendous and unforeseen social, economic, and political problems.

There is little question that there are many political dissidents among these people, individuals whose lives are threatened and who are justified in seeking asylum. Many Kurds, Iranians, Iraqis, and others have political reasons to seek refuge in some of the democratic Western countries. Their numbers, however, are small when compared with the number of individuals who seek asylum for economic reasons.

When the Eastern European countries were freed from communism, particularly when this occurred in the USSR, the majority of the people in the Western world experienced a sense of euphoria and celebrated the victory of winning the Cold War. The excitement of the West Germans was particularly overwhelming; at last, East Germany and West Germany were united. Although the rest of the Western world was relieved that they would no longer live under the threat of the Soviet's nuclear threat, the Germans were dreaming of the renaissance of Germany as a future superpower, one that not only would dominate the European community but also would surpass Japan and be on a par with the United States. It was not long before reality and soberness replaced the initial euphoria.

The West Germans had a great deal of empathy and compassion for the desperate desires of their brethren on the opposite side of the wall. The East Germans were extremely anxious to enjoy some of the goods and prosperity that were so easily available to the West Germans but that had been sorely lacking on the Eastern side. In the beginning, the West Germans even provided their Eastern brothers with money to buy the items they had so long wished to possess and were pleased to provide the opportunity for the Easterners to enjoy a new level of prosperity.

Soon, however, the dreamed of unification became a nightmare. The West German government imposed a 7 percent unification tax, which every working person and entrepreneur had to pay. This would have been tolerable, as would have the influx of the East Germans, the Poles, Czechs, Rumanians, and other emigrants seeking economic gain, had it been simply a case of losing a job to a Pole here or an apartment to a Czech there. However, the West Germans began to feel threatened, then outraged, when they realized that their social and economic systems were in jeopardy. Their discontent was further fueled with the realization that their country, which had once been known for law and order, was rapidly moving to a state of chaos.

Their change of heart did not occur because some political dissidents were momentarily benefitting from the liberal laws of the country. It happened because the West Germans did not want to carry the burden of unification.

The East Germans were, at the same time, aggravated that the unification did not bring them any immediate advantage; on the contrary, it contributed to massive unemployment in their part of the country.

Suddenly, these people faced a variety of problems, not the least of which included feelings of inferiority to their Western brothers and the fact that they suddenly had to work very hard and compete to make a living, a situation with which they were not familiar. Finally, neither of the two German groups could tolerate the influx of refugees from the Third World countries.

This latter consideration forced them to work harder and give up even more for refugees with whom they had nothing in common; race, language, culture, and religion were all different. Although the majority of the refugees from the Third World were happy to have a place to live and hope for a better future, many of them got involved in illegal activities, such as drug trafficking and the importation of illegal immigrants. Both activities provided high monetary gain for the enterprising groups involved.

The flood of East European immigrants did not help to lower the tension. They not only placed additional burdens on the social and economic systems, they also contributed to the disorder in the country. Criminality and robbery reached the highest level ever known in Germany. The revolts of the Skinheads are only one expression of the resultant outrage. As proud as the German people are and as hesitant as they are to admit to error, many of the West Germans would have raised the wall twice as high, had they known the outcome of the German unification and the liberating of the Eastern European countries.

The situation in Germany is nothing new or unique; all Western European countries are having their share of problems, and the United States is not much different. Many Cubans and Haitians have sought political asylum in the United States, especially in the early 1990s, but just as many have sought asylum for the economic benefits of a better life. The poverty and deprivation of their own countries have driven them to risk their lives, and those of their families, to go through the dangerous attempts necessary to achieve a better future in the United States.

The developments following the disintegration of the former USSR are equally interesting. There was immediate enthusiasm in the academic and industrial circles of the United States and Western European countries. Leaders in these areas envisioned a brain drain from the Soviet Union of the most highly qualified scientists, which would help to bring new blood into the areas of research and development and provide a relatively cheap source of scientific expertise. The politicians may have foreseen another cause for satisfaction: the relocation of former Soviet scientists would neutralize the former foe, leaving them in no position to present a threat to the Western world.

This enthusiasm may well be short-lived. Following the immigration of the scientists, it is only natural to assume there will be an immigration of the more typical Soviet burgers wanting to achieve a better economic future in the United States and other industrialized countries of the West. The picture becomes even more bleak when one considers the Poles, Czechs, and other populations seeking a better life. If this potential is not available in their own countries, they will use every means possible to relocate to a country where the possibility exists. As to the complacency of the politicians, their feeling of well-being may be short-lived and ill-advised. Scientists for whom the United States and Europe may have little use could well end up in countries such as Iran or Iraq, assisting in their attempts to attain supremacy and gain access to nuclear bombs and similar destructive weapons systems.

Is anything being done to prevent this future scenario? Very little, unfortunately. The rich nations of the West are providing some monetary support in an effort to ease the worst of the burdens, but little is being done to protect and assist the common people of the suffering nations while industry and power leaders attempt to sort things out in their own best interest. The fact is that Russia and other republics of the former USSR are rich in fossil energy and other raw materials and do not need to go through a long period of economic and political upheaval before managing their own economies. Why should the Russians — who have the largest gold reserves in the world and plenty of crude oil — suffer hunger and a cold winter? Because, until the long-term advantages for the politicians and big boys of industry are worked out, there will be no attempts to alleviate the suffering of the people. Once those advantages are secured, the people will be doomed to hard work to benefit these leaders.

The situation will be little different than it was during the Cold War. Then, it was the military-industrial complexes in both hemispheres who called the shots. To reach their goals, the Soviet military threat was created and presented as much more critical than it was. Had the Soviets been observed objectively and wisely, one could not have missed the fact that they represented a hollow threat.

One had only to look closely at the former East Germany, the most-developed country in the Eastern Bloc, to realize that in spite of their collective military manpower and weapons, their economy would not last long, due to their inferior manufacturing methods and the shortage of all kinds of goods. It was only a matter of time until their economy would have been exhausted. Unlike the strong, radical fanaticism of Islam, whose believers would willing commit collective suicide by attacking superior Western industrialized countries, the Marxist ideology was not that strong. Nevertheless, the perceived threat helped the military-industrial complex of the Western world — particularly the United States and the former USSR — to prosper beyond imagination for decades, at the expense of other industries.

In retrospect, the people who believed we were facing a major threat and who worked hard to prevent such a threat, may well feel cheated, realizing that the former Soviet military menace was only a paper tiger. These same people may experience a feeling of outrage to find that hamburgers from McDonald's have more power over Soviet generals than Grumman's F-14 jet fighters. With the introduction of McDonald's to Moscow's Red Square, two Soviet generals and other officers were placed in charge of establishing order among the long lines of customers. The power of the hamburger should not come as any surprise. Hamburgers feed the stomach; guns kill people. When the stomach is full, people are usually afraid of guns. When the stomachs are empty and the body is pursuing a slow, gradual course of starvation, guns and death are not nearly as frightening. Had the U.S. politicians realized just how much power a McDonald's restaurant could wield, the Pentagon could have saved hundreds of trillions of dollars on armaments and the world would have been a safer and friendlier place for all inhabitants.

What can be done to prevent repeating previous errors? The simplest and most rational approach would be to help improve the standard of living in all countries where people are under severe economic pressure, forced to leave their countries and seek refuge in the industrialized Western nations. This task could be accomplished by effectively exporting and creating jobs in those countries.

Would this stop the emmigration attempts of the people of those nations? Would this measure harm the economy of the country that is exporting the jobs? The majority of the immigrants who are motivated by severe economic pressure would probably remain in their homeland and avoid the unknown hardship of adjusting to a new host country. People are inclined to live in a society with which they are accustomed, where people share the same language, religion, cultural background, and customs. Providing a way for them to realize economic advantages in their own country combined with a tightening of current liberal immigration laws would reduce the flow of immigrants to a trickle.

As to the concern for the country exporting the work, the success of this venture and its effect on the country's economy would be largely dependent on the way this is done. If the concept of environomics is applied to the manufacture of superior products and the job-exporting country receives its compensation through superior products and profits, it will, in fact, remain a matter of rearrangement and distribution in that country. Initially, the population of the job-exporting country will receive superior products. From a global standpoint, the flow of goods to the primary country would be compensated by a monetary flow toward the secondary country, and this flows back to the primary country in the form of profit.

As the demand for a particular product reaches the point of saturation in the primary country and demand slows, the product would be used as an export to other nations. At this point, more and more money would return to the primary country in the form of profits, contributing to the trade surplus. This profit could be used to implement the same process with other products in other countries.

The question is, how do we provide full employment in the primary country? This can be done by improving and increasing capabilities and productivity in the areas of service, leisure, research, and development. As more and more people are released from the manufacturing sectors, they would move to these other sectors or have more time for leisure. Increased leisure time frequently leads to advances in research and development.

This approach would generate income for these people to buy imported goods, until a point of saturation is reached. In addition, this approach will contribute to the improvement of existing products, technology, and methods of production. The future source of prosperity would be secured.

This method would produce positive results for both groups of countries. It will reduce the flow of immigrants significantly and prevent environmentally destructive activities that are now pursued in a simple effort to survive. It would also contribute to the political, economic, social, and environmental stability of the world. It is imperative that the rich nations of the world begin to replace their exploitive activities in Third World countries with constructive efforts.

Ironically, the entire economy of a nation stands or falls with the level of employment. This is particularly true of the market-oriented economies of the industrialized Western nations. The closer a nation moves to full employment, the more positive is the economy of that country. The higher the unemployment rate, the closer the country moves toward recession. People who are employed are people who spend money, it is as simple as that. This spending leads to a higher demand for production, and that leads to more employment. As long as the economy shows an upward trend, there is little to worry about, other than inflation.

It is my intention not to describe the concept of the business cycle but to question why full employment, in the conventional sense, is the guarantor for an economic boom. Such an approach requires that we produce more, buy more, destroy more, then start the cycle over again. If this destructive process can be managed without interruption, full employment and economic boom levels will continue to exist. However, we know that this cannot continue indefinitely, not so much because of past experience but because of the facts presented in this book.

Why must people continue to work in the conventional sense to maintain a cycle of work-buy-destroy-replace? Why not create a world where people work to satisfy their needs only once, rather than again and again? Is the prevailing equation between employment and economic booms the ultimate wisdom? Could it not be modified in a manner that could prevent economic ups and downs on the one side and environmental destruction on the other side?

The cumulative economic-political errors of the past have run our economy aground, and it appears that conventional measures — an influx of money and reducing the interest rates, for example — are not going to solve the problems of the 1990–1992 recession. At best, these measures may help us crawl slowly and painfully out of the recession, without experiencing the remarkable results of previous economic cycles.

The fact is that when a nation and the majority of the middle class working people are overly indebted, any additional income goes to pay the debts or service the interest on those debts. This leaves little or no money to be spent on new goods and services, which is what is required to stimulate the economy. Until we find a rational approach to this problem and implement it rigorously, the economy will remain sluggish.

Impulsive economic and politically motivated measures produce only a short-term result. With the errors of the past, the economy has been programmed for a sluggish trend. If unemployment continues to grow and the fear of unemployment threatens additional members of the population, the current situation will be further compounded by negative trends. People will be inclined to spend no more than absolutely necessary for basic requirements. Any measure to stimulate the economy to additional buying will fail. Seeking to correct the existing economic problems through application of an already-failed concept is not an effective solution.

Industrialized nations of the world will be forced to search for new avenues to resolve their economic problems. Whether they go this path voluntarily is the only question. Sooner or later, their choices will be limited. They will be forced to seek new answers, due to limits imposed on them through economic, political, social, and environmental realities.

How many more automobiles can be produced to stimulate the economy without running out of space for those automobiles? Already, cars have filled most of the streets in many of the European cities, such as West Berlin, Hamburg, Frankfurt am Main, Amsterdam, London, and Paris, as well as numerous others. In most of the streets in these cities, cars are parked in double rows, one row on the pavement and the second row on the side of the road, leaving just enough space for each car to get out of the parking space. This has resulted in two-lane streets being reduced to one lane for driving. When drivers meet from opposite directions, one must yield to the other, bringing traffic to a total stop. Many cities are closing more and more streets in downtown areas to automobile traffic and restricting the areas to pedestrian traffic. Amsterdam is considering becoming the first city in the world to prohibit cars from entering the city. Many big cities in the United States are considering such an approach, even though the situation here is not yet that critical.

Not all industrial products have reached the saturation level of the automobile. There is no doubt we have some way to go before the same condition exists for televisions, telephones, washing machines, dishwashers, and the like. Still, one must realize that the method of quantitative growth cannot function indefinitely as a vehicle to stimulate the economy. There are three reasons for this.

First, the economy will eventually crumble under the interest costs, which make paying for goods take longer than the life of the item purchased and drive up the cost of replacement goods. Second, we will reach environmental limits. Third, we will deplete the raw materials and energy necessary to drive such an economy.

How much longer can the pollution of water, air, and land caused by our diversified economic activities be tolerated? How many people in a household can be put to work to pay for goods that are no longer functional? How can people who have lost their jobs pay their current obligations, let alone maintain their homes and families? How much longer will our raw materials and fossil energy sources, such as crude oil, last with the exploitive activities in which we are engaged? It is becoming clear that conventional economic wisdom cannot provide a long-term remedy to the economic ills through quantitative economic growth.

If the conventional method will not work, what is the answer? In order to implement the concept of environomics, it is imperative that we prevent waste in every manner. Because we used the example of the automobile earlier, we will continue to use that item here. It is one of the critical issues facing many of the countries and an issue with which people are concerned, in one way or another.

There is no doubt that we must have a means of transportation from one location to another. Once people experience the pleasure of freedom of movement, it is an advantage they will not forsake. This book does not endorse any particular method of transportation but hopes to provide guidelines for the necessary behaviors regarding the objective of movement, whether it be by automobile or mass transit.

Assuming the automobile remains a major choice for transportation, how do we deal with the problems related to cars, especially from the standpoint of rational behavior and waste prevention? Consider the main problems directly inherent with the automobile:

*   Death and injuries due to accidents,
*   Air and noise pollution in the cities and on the highways,
*   High density of cars and slow traffic,
*   Space requirements for parking cars,
*   Inefficiency and resultant waste of energy to fuel cars, and
*   Strain on raw materials and fossil energy sources.

When these points are considered, it is clear that the future for any kind of traffic — air, mass transit, automobile — will be determined by our success in eliminating the pollution caused by this traffic and finding alternative energy sources to power the engines. In the case of the automobile, if their useful life is extended in high-density cities, the problem of space must be seriously dealt with. Otherwise, the current trend in manufacturing larger cars, which are inefficient from an energy standpoint and highly polluting from an environmental standpoint, will bring an end to the era of automobiles.

Two features must be integrated into the manufacture of future automobiles. The cars must become smaller, which would reduce the above-mentioned problems considerably. Each car on today's roads is occupied by an average of 1.3 persons. Two-seater cars, instead of four-seater cars, would serve the needs of much of the population and result in more space available for parking.

Future cars must be built following the concept of environomics, which requires a longer life span, increased durability, and integration of prosperity inducing technology (PIT) and modular design. A smaller car with these characteristics would increase the chances of automobiles remaining as a major means of individual transportation in the future, and those automobiles would not have the current negative impact on the environment, raw materials, and energy. All of these factors would contribute to the general prosperity.

There is no question that implementation of these characteristics will require some time. Until then, we must deal with two issues: the harm caused by existing cars and the transition period until the new generation of cars is available.

There is little that can be done with existing automobiles. One possibility is to convert them from gasoline, a polluting energy, to gas, an environmentally friendly energy source that is almost nonpolluting. There is no major technical obstacle nor any substantive cost associated with this conversion, which is practical and economical. The City Gas Company of Florida has converted all gasoline-powered vehicles owned by the company to gas-powered vehicles.

The issues of the transition period must be handled with foresight and prudence. Unnecessary or ineffective experiments must be avoided. The electric car, which is powered by energy from nuclear power plants, is not an effective solution, for instance. A car is as environmentally safe as its source of energy, and we know the dangers of the nuclear plants. The involved industries need to begin working together in a concerted effort to implement the concept of environomics in the automobile industry.

One of the major stumbling blocks to this issue is the fact that the automobile industry is currently profitable and will not be easily convinced to effect changes that are going to cost money. Government is often slow to react to, and slower to require implementation of, changes that will affect the special-interest groups that put politicians in office. What can the average citizen do to get the system out of the current deadlock?

Changes must take place in several areas of our political and economic systems if we are to improve these and make them more efficient and fair. Restructuring our political system is as important as restructuring our economic approach.

Congress — both the House and the Senate — must reflect a wider diversity of professions, as opposed to its current makeup of mainly lawyers. The law must be written, but lawyers do not have the answers to the wide diversity of problems facing the country — issues of health care, education, economy, banking, foreign affairs, agriculture, and the like. If we want to bring substance and real change, in the interest of increasing the efficiency and effectiveness of Congress, we need to elect experts from all fields of life — economists, accountants, farmers, doctors, engineers, environmentalists, and business people, not just attorneys.

A limit should be set for Congressional terms, opening the potential for younger generations, with newer ideas and ideals, to determine political events. The need for this change is already being felt and, in some areas, implemented.

A system must be created that does not allow the politicians to become obligated to the various special-interest groups for purposes of getting elected and remaining in office. Often, funds received from these groups are based on the promise of favors to be granted once the candidate is in office. That fact prevents the candidate from being objective in making political decisions. The easiest way to halt this practice is to pass a federal law prohibiting receipt of funds and donations from any kind of business, regardless of size. At the same time, certain limits should be applied to donations from private individuals and private sources and use of the candidate's private funds. This would help limit the potential of rich candidates and candidates with wealthy supporters and friends to acquire political positions as a sole result of excessive spending on advertising and media exposure. The desired result is that individuals would be elected because of the substance of their political message, as opposed to the amount of money spent.

Further, a ban must be put on the current practice of allowing members of Congress to benefit from travels financed by special interests or accepting honoraria from special-interest groups. Quite simply, any financial or material incentives that could corrupt or influence incumbent and future politicians should be made unlawful. In addition, a limit must be set on campaign spending, and matching government funds should be eliminated entirely.

The government's only interest in promoting candidates should be to assure that all candidates enjoy the same media exposure, so the voting population will know the goals and programs of all who are running. This would allow the U.S. people to make a decision based on the merits, knowledge, and political goals of each candidate. Currently, many voters are influenced by the distorted and massive advertising campaigns of candidates with rich friends and seemingly limitless campaign funds. Equity in exposure would result in better informed, more objective voters.

Although planned economies have been a failure in many of the former Communist countries, having no plan is an equally sure path to disaster. Every political party and each incumbent politician has an agenda. Inevitably, reaching the goals of that agenda seems to rely on taxation, either increasing current taxes or implementing new taxes to fund their projects. In doing so, the government creates the features of a planned economy and becomes the entrepreneur at the same time. The best way to realize governmental plans for such issues as health care, education, and energy is to have the private sector, the business entrepreneurs, actively participate. For this to work, the government must have a precise plan and a process for its implementation.

If the project is something new or if it exists on a small scale, the government could stimulate entrepreneurial efforts by offering long-term tax incentives attractive enough to truly appeal to the private sector. Although the government would initially lose the tax revenue, the positive effect would be the creation of more jobs, which would generate revenue from the employees' income tax. In addition, there is no actual loss, because the entrepreneurial company would not exist without the tax incentives.

To stimulate or improve an existing industry, an increase in the purchase of its products or service must be initiated. One of the easiest ways to do this is to provide easy financing to the consumers. Interest rates must be reduced to the lowest level possible, perhaps even be eliminated for a short time. Consideration could be given to providing tax incentives to financial institutions who provide such low-interest funds. This would create more consumers, which would create more jobs and maintain existing jobs. Again, the benefits would accrue through the additional income tax revenues that would be paid by the workers.

A successful transition from a wasteful, destructive economy and society with irrational behavior to a prudent economy and society based on the concept of environomics is necessary. Until this occurs, we must do everything possible to prevent irrational behavior and waste and to conserve and save as much as possible. The post-environomics economy and society will reward us with a general prosperity, in real terms, within a safe environment.

In the interest of achieving these goals, I have provided below the ten rules for achieving a post-environomics economy and society — a true utopia.

1. The post-environomic society — heaven or utopia, whichever term you prefer — can be realized on earth. Each of us shall help to create it.
2. The people of the earth shall recognize the damage and destruction they have created and shall clean up the planet and return it to its previous pristine condition.

3. The people of the earth shall not exploit or destroy nature or her resources but shall handle these with care.

4. Wealth is in the general prosperity of the people and not in their exploitation. Smaller is better; it provides you with your share and lets others have theirs.

5. The people of the earth shall strive for qualitative growth and keep quantitative growth within limits.

6. The people of the earth shall strive to develop and implement PITs, avoiding prosperity decreasing technologies forever.

7. The people of the earth shall integrate more modular concepts in design and production of technical products.

8. The people of the earth shall design products employing minimal and/or economic use of raw materials and fossil energy. They shall use, as much as possible, recycled materials.

9. The people of the earth shall shun and eliminate centralized power plants.

10. All energy facilities shall be decentralized as much as possible, and their sources shall be renewable energy.

12

Prudent and Constructive
Economic and Political Measures

The economic situation of the average household has been steadily worsening over the last few decades. In spite of the promises made by politicians in regard to their concern and their plans for the welfare of the average citizen, the outcome of the measures they institute to realize these promised goals is in direct contradiction of their campaign pledges.

It was not that long ago that one salary could support the average household, but today, this is no longer true. A number of surveys have revealed that in most cases, it is now necessary for two people, sometimes three, in the household to work, to maintain the same standard of living. Those homes where there is only one salary are forced to lower their standard of living to get by.

How did this occur? Chapters 10 and 11 have described many of the problems. In short, it would be safe to say our current situation is the result of a lack of prudent and constructive economic-political measures, due to lack of knowledge and experience on the part of our politicians or to the influence exercised by the lobbyists of powerful special-interest groups. These factors have contributed to the exploitation of the people by elected officials who are not fulfilling their mandate nor serving the people who elected them. The end result of the many negative actions taken over the past years is that the U.S. people have little money to spend and less money to save. In the early 1990s, it is estimated that the average U.S. household has 87 percent of its disposable income precommitted to expenses, such as mortgages, car payments, and credit card purchases. That leaves only 13 percent for new or additional expenses or for savings. It is no wonder that Americans cannot save.

It is my intent not to present in this chapter a summary of all the economic ills and unfair practices plaguing our economy but to offer a few examples of specific problems and potential solutions.

Much has been written about the growing disparity between the rich and the poor in the United States. There has been a disproportional increase in the incomes of business magnates compared with the salaries of the average worker. In 1960, the growth ratio was 12 to 1; in 1988, that difference increased, reflecting a ratio of 93 to 1. The 1990s saw further increases, with unfair tax cuts favoring the wealthy and, at the same time, burdening the country's middle class. That period saw further negative trends, evidenced by the exploitive practices of banks and retail stores in charging interest rates on purchases that approached the level of usury, the lack of health insurance for more than 34 million Americans, and a health care system that has little to recommend it to the average individual, to name a few of the economic ills. Coupled with the economic problems are the social and political problems. We have seen an increase in the illegal use of drugs, criminal activities, racial disturbances, and the number of school dropouts. Many of these problems are the direct or indirect result of the economic problems facing much of our population. One has to ask why the average worker has been placed in such an awkward and detrimental economic situation, particularly when the opposite could be achieved with prudent and constructive economic-political measures.

The dilemma surrounding the recession of the early 1990s and the lack of recovery that we previously experienced from such an economic downturn is that no measure appears to be working effectively, although there is no shortage of suggestions for recovery. However, many of the measures that have worked in the past (reducing the interest rate, for example) have had no effect on the current economy. Part of this is due to the greed of the individuals and organizations who refuse to pass such reductions on to their customers.

The Federal Reserve discount rate — the rate the Feds charge banks for short-term loans — was 4.5 percent at the end of 1991, the lowest it has been in 19 years. However, strapped banks did not pass the reductions to all borrowers. Auto loans dropped only marginally, and credit card rates remained practically unchanged at 20 percent and more.

Various groups of politicians, economists, advisors, commentators, and journalists are proposing suggestions for a fast recovery of the economy, hoping to bring us out of the recession. Many of these suggestions start with tax cuts and tax credits and extend to capital spending, based on Keynesian fiscal policy. Although these and other similar economic-political measures may have some positive impact on stimulating the economy, arbitrary measures could lack the desired long-term effects. At best, this could provide mixed results.

To get a clearer idea of what such measures may accomplish, it is necessary to explore the pros and cons. A tax cut, regardless of the manner in which it was applied, would be of little, if any, help to an unemployed individual with no source of income. Those individuals who are working would probably divert any tax savings toward reducing or servicing their current debts, which are extensive in too many cases. This would not contribute to stimulating the economy, as the money would go toward items already purchased.

An investment tax credit would permit businesses to subtract a percentage of the money they invest in plants and machinery directly from their tax bills. On the positive side, this would encourage expansion and generate new jobs and a stronger economy. On the negative side, such a measure would reward businesses for investments they would have made even without the incentive. In addition, it would help capital-intensive industries more than labor-intensive firms and would benefit established companies more than start-up business, which would truly be creating new jobs. Attempts to stimulate the economy through deficit spending have already resulted in a federal debt of over $3 trillion, according to official figures.

In summation, arbitrary tax incentives may provide a quick fix for the economy, but the effects would be of short-term nature and would lead to excesses in the economy; after a short-term upward trend, the economy would fall back to its initial stagnating condition. The end result of this policy would be additional social costs and an unnecessary burdening or destruction of the ecology. Examples of this shallow and arbitrary economic-political measure can be seen in the myriad of empty office buildings, shopping malls, and luxury houses across the country.

Tax incentives must fulfill two primary economic goals. First, they must help the threatened industry sectors make themselves more competitive in the marketplace by retooling, restructuring, and improving techniques, in order at least to maintain their market position and to provide jobs as long as a continued demand for the products and/or services exists. They must also help protect these industries from foreign competition. Second, the incentives must promote those sectors of industry in which there is a great demand for their products and services at an economically satisfactory price. The sectors of industry where we see a current and critical need include health care, energy, and housing for the average U.S. family.

As none of these standard measures appear to be the solution, where do we find an answer? To find an effective answer, it is imperative that we concentrate our thoughts and objectives on the proper goals. The very first concern with the economy is of a short-term nature — we must implement measures to keep the economy afloat until the long-term goals can be smoothly and easily realized. The long-term goal is, of course, the implementation of the concept of environomics, as outlined in this book. However, many of the ideas contained in the environomics concept can be applied to boosting the economy in the short-term as well.

Before we can select even short-term economic-political measures to address the issue, it is critical that some basic corrective course be taken to get the economy back on the right track. One of the first steps is to correct erroneous economic data, information that is being used to calculate and provide inaccurate figures regarding our economy.

The inflation rate figures are an excellent example. The Bureau of Labor Statistics tracks the prices of 100,000 items per month, but their figures do not reflect the true inflation rate; this is because they changed the accounting rules in the early 1980s. Automobiles, for example, are no longer counted. The reasoning behind this change was that new models always have improvements so that even though the price goes up each year, you cannot compare this year's car with last year's car. A similar decision was made regarding mortgages because although 66 percent of the U.S. people have mortgages, not everyone does. Have such changes altered the picture very much? Absolutely. If the automobile and mortgage figures, as well as other items that were dropped, were included in the calculation of the inflation rates, the true inflation rates would probably be three times higher than they appear today. This should come as no surprise to anyone who compares what a dollar will buy at the grocery store today.

The same false picture is reflected in the method of calculating the unemployment rate. If the definition of joblessness is broadened to include those who wanted jobs but were not job hunting and those who held jobs but still suffered the concerns usually associated with unemployment, some labor economists contend that the unemployment rate in the United States in November of 1991 would have been more than 12 million, or nearly 10 percent of the labor force. The official numbers, using the inaccurate calculation method, showed figures of 8.5 million and 6.8 percent unemployment.

The situation is compounded by the uncertainty that haunts the future of individuals and our economy. This uncertainty could neutralize the effects of any measure implemented to improve economic conditions. The fact is that private, corporate, and government debts are ballooning, and someone has to finance them. Add to this the issues of the savings and loans bailouts, the AIDS epidemic threat, the anticipated insurance fiasco, environmental concerns and cleanup, and needed reforms in the health care system, and one can see that it is absurd to expect inflation to decline.

If we are going to deal with these and other problems (and they must be dealt with), we must not only identify the problems but also attempt to identify the tasks involved in correcting the financial, social, and political burdens we face. This gloomy picture of the economy, coupled with the escalating environmental problems we face, gives reason for despair. However, as severe as the situation may be, it is not yet totally out of control and should not be cause for resignation and acceptance. A drastic and effective change can be initiated if the economic-political measures used are based on a prudent and constructive manner of thinking.

One example of implementing prudent and constructive measures would be provision of tax credits or tax cuts to *selected* business, rather than arbitrarily implementing such a measure across the board. This would assist the government in realizing its goals for the economy. Such credits and cuts would be provided to a few limited industries, and the multiplicator effect would trigger a boost in other industry sectors.

The first step would be to provide these measures to the health care and energy industries, as described in previous chapters, which would be a move toward bringing sanity to the economy and would stimulate the economy immediately by creating new jobs. In addition, as majority of the population would soon experience an improvement in their standard of living and quality of life.

A second step would deal with the manner of financing home mortgages. Rechanneling Social Security money toward shortening the financing period of home mortgages would provide strong stimulation to the economy. There can be little doubt that creating the possibility for more people to own their own home and to pay off the mortgage in a much shorter period of time — 15 years instead of 30 years, for example — is a sound and constructive policy. People would own their house in the earlier stages of their lives, providing a material form of social security, and in the long run, the Social Security fund would be strengthened. Such a measure would immediately stimulate the housing market and, as an indirect result, the entire economy, without any need for deficit spending. The only change would be in the disposition of Social Security funds for a temporary period of time. After the home mortgage is paid off, the payments would revert back to the Social Security fund until the temporarily diverted funds were brought up to date.

Before exploring this possibility, it is necessary to provide a brief explanation of the idea behind Social Security and how the system works and then examine the current practices in mortgage financing.

In *Social Security: The System That Works*, Merton and Joan Bernstein wrote:

> Sooner or later, most of us will need retirement income. The good news is that we can depend on Social Security benefits to be there when we need them. Social Security benefits alone, however, will not enable most to maintain their accustomed living standards after retirement. So supplementation is needed, either from private plans, savings, or a more generous Social Security program; otherwise many will face declining living standards throughout their older years. The bad news is that other retirement income plans are surprisingly less dependable. Many participants won't get benefits; for those who do, benefits will be degraded by inflation.
>
> While the great majority of Americans register their support for Social Security, many express doubt that the system will meet its obligations in the next century. Some also express concern that, even if Social Security does make good on its promises, future beneficiaries will not get as good a deal as their parents and grandparents did. Some, especially the affluent, believe that they could do better on their own, that, unencumbered by mandatory Social Security payroll taxes, they could invest like amounts more advantageously.

The idea here is not to degrade the Social Security system, challenge its validity, or suggest a substitute that might be better than the existing system. As these authors point out in their book, one should not worry about the collapse of the Social Security System; it is as secure as it could possibly be. Nevertheless, the bitter fact remains that if one depends solely on Social Security income for support during retirement, the chances are very high that there is going to be a decline in the living standard. That is the concern we wish to address here and for which we propose a solution that will at least partially maintain individuals' standard of living when the time comes that they must depend on Social Security for their income.

Home ownership early in life would be the greatest single contribution to an individual's financial security. To reduce the length of time necessary for paying off a home mortgage, thus greatly reducing the amount of interest required, a portion of the total Social Security tax on an individual's wages could be diverted to reduce the principal balance of the mortgage on a primary residence.

The two major components of every mortgage payment are principal and interest. In Chapter 10, we discussed the role of interest and interest rates in the economy and the adverse effects on the economy. Stimulating the economy without resolving the problems caused by interest and interest rates is practically impossible. Were we to return to the lower interest rates of the 1950s and 1960s, when rates were no more than 3 percent, there would be little, if any, damage to the economy. We know, from the analysis we did in a previous chapter, that the effects of interest and interest rates on the economy are negative. We also know that the interest rate presents the characteristics of exponential growth. The higher the interest rates, the more extreme are their negative effects on the economy.

The current practices of calculating and dictating payment schedules for loans by banks and financial institutions has significantly reduced the purchasing power of the U.S. people, eliminating the opportunity for many people to buy homes or high-ticket items. In addition, the payment schedules currently in use enslave people financially for a period that exceeds the useful life of the item purchased. Whether one is talking about a house, a car, furniture, or appliances, it is not uncommon for the purchaser to be repaying borrowed monies long after expenditures for repair and replacements have become necessary or the item has become obsolete. Such expenditures further burden the purchaser and necessitate the use of savings or the borrowing of additional monies. One of the primary concerns regarding current repayment policies is the initial application of most of the payment toward interest costs, with only a negligible amount going to reduce the principal of the loan. Purchasers are often surprised to discover that after several years of payments, the amount owed on principal has not been reduced significantly.

This leaves little doubt that the employment of interest and interest rates in the current manner results in exploitation of the people and the economy. The fatal consequences of this financing policy cannot be ignored. Unfortunately, few people are truly aware of the manner in which payments are calculated and applied and do not realize they are being robbed blind by the existing practices. The current loan amortization programs allow the banks and financial institutions to collect large quantities over a long period of time. To further swell profits, closing costs that represent a percentage of the loan amount are collected by these institutions to "pay their operating expenses."

The rationalization for the exorbitant interest paid on home mortgages is that this interest can be deducted from an individual's income tax, thus compensating for the large amounts that are not applied to principal. Although such a tax deduction is a benefit of owning a home instead of renting one, mortgage interest is not a tax shelter. Not every dollar out of your pocket can be deducted directly from the amount of income tax you owe. Even in the highest federal income tax bracket, 33 percent, your loss on interest paid on your home mortgage is 67 cents on the dollar.

How can one reduce the amount of interest that flows to the financial institution? Actually, if the monthly payment is increased by less than 20 percent, a 30-year mortgage would be paid off in half the time. It is usually recommended that an amount equal to the next month's principal be paid with the regular monthly payment. This is where the money diverted from Social Security could be used to shorten the length of the mortgage. Once the mortgage is paid off — which would occur in much less time than currently required — the mortgage dollars would be available and could be used to pay back the Social Security fund.

There are several positive effects that recommend this policy. People would own their home in a shorter period of time, with less of their disposable income going toward servicing the interest on the loan. The funds temporarily diverted from the Social Security fund would flow back into the fund without effort, the monthly payment simply going to the fund instead of the mortgage. Individuals would have more disposable income available for additional purchases over the standard mortgage period of 30 years.

In other words, once the mortgage is paid off, a few more monthly payments would reimburse the Social Security system. At that point, the homeowner could accumulate or spend the equivalent of 15 or 20 years' worth of house payments. A tax policy would be formulated to assure that most of the money was saved, guaranteeing securing retirement for the individual and capital for the economy.

There are two more benefits to this approach: it would permit people to retire earlier, creating further employment opportunities for the balance of the population and improving the quality of life in our older years, and more people would be in a position to afford a home, thus stimulating the construction industry and other related areas of the economy.

The most-negative potential effect of this policy would be the threat of rising inflation. This could be regulated by controlling the construction market through the gradual implementation of using Social Security monies to reduce mortgage principal.

This policy would also be successfully applied as a solution to existing vacant houses. Although it would not directly create jobs in the new-home construction market, it would make it possible for many more families to own their own homes and would boost the economy indirectly through its multiplicator effects.

Although it may be a controversial view and against much conventional economic wisdom, increased inflation could be controlled or avoided if the Federal Reserve Bank would reduce its interest rates to a minimum and require lending institutions to do the same. The ramifications of such an action would be widespread and effective. The interest rate in the United States would be reduced to a point substantially lower than the prevailing interest rates in other major currencies, such as those of Japan, Germany, France, and Great Britain. This measure would contribute to the fluctuation of the dollar and its conversion to other currencies with higher interest rates. That action, in turn, would take the money out of circulation in the United States and neutralize the possibility of a rise in inflation while contributing to the gradual devaluation of the dollar against other currencies.

This measure would stimulate the export potential of U.S. goods, which would cause dollars to flow back to the United States as payment. Because the interest rates in the United States would be much lower than those in the other countries, the dollar would seek its way back to currencies that yield higher interest. As this cycle repeated itself, other countries would follow the same route and reduce their interest rates to the level of that in the United States.

This approach would result in several advantages for the country. Until other countries instituted countermeasures, the economy would be stimulated. The export industry would experience tremendous growth. A trade surplus would develop, and foreign goods would have a hard time competing in the U.S. domestic market because of the devaluation of the dollar in comparison with their currencies.

The negative effects on the economy from lowering the interest rates should be negligible. Other than the fluctuation and devaluation of the dollar and the flow of dollars to other countries with higher interest rates, there should be no major concerns. The chances are good that this would not happen to such a degree that government intervention would be required. If a critical situation did arise, the Federal Reserve Bank would be responsible for assuring that the volume of money in circulation was adequately maintained to prevent the economy from falling back into stagnation.

We cannot emphasize too strongly that the first place to begin implementing prudent and constructive economic-political measures is with a reduction of the negative effects of interest and interest rates on the domestic economy. As stated before, the interest rate must be reduced to

a minimum. The best policy to boost the economy would be the elimination of interest, at least temporarily, and provision of interest-free
financing. This would stimulate the economy by encouraging people to
make new purchases.

As a side effect, lower interest rates could potentially save the U.S.
government payments on the national debt. For instance, in fiscal 1991,
the $286 billion in interest payments on the national debt represented 20
percent of the $1.4 trillion federal budget. For fiscal 1992, the Treasury
Department estimated it would pay $304 billion in interest on the national
debt. Lower interest rates could save the U.S. government $200 billion
or more per year in interest payments or debt obligations.

However, interest-free financing should not be implemented arbitrarily
but should concentrate on domestic industries, such as solar energy. This
would create new jobs and new opportunities, providing income to
stimulate the economy.

In addition, the problems resulting from previous purchases that have
overburdened the majority of the population financially must be dealt
with. The best solution would be to free the people from excess payments
that result from the high interest currently charged on mortgages, loans,
and credit card purchases. The practice of calculating interest on a daily
basis and applying compound interest to home mortgages or other loans
is extremely detrimental to the average homeowner and prospective
homebuyer; it is critical that interest be calculated as simple interest and
not compounded on a daily or any other arbitrary time basis.

Why do financial institutions follow the existing practices, and how
would changing these practices affect the institutions?

Banks and other financial institutions are just like any other commercial
enterprise. They want and need credit-worthy customers. Once money
has been loaned to these customers, the institution wants to keep them as
customers for as long as possible. The leaders in the financial industry,
those people who make policy decisions, are much better equipped to
deal with the intricacies of finance and accounting methods than the
average individual, who does not have an extensive education or practical
background in the manipulation of numbers and the development of
calculation methods. Financial leaders are adept at developing and
designing financing plans that will increase the profit of their particular
institution and their own income. These are the people who designed the
current amortization schedule, which forces the debtor to pay the interest
first, leaving the large principal balance almost untouched for the majority
of the loan; after the bulk of the interest has been collected, the principal
begins to be reduced.

Banks and other financial institutions want to lend out all their money, just as a retail merchant wishes to sell all of the stock. If this is the primary goal, the rate of interest should make no difference, as long as the rate on money they lend is higher than the rate of interest on money they borrow. Actually, banks would be more inclined to lend out money at a lower rate when their income is determined by the difference between the two rates, because a lower rate of interest will attract more business. Consequently, there is little, if any, reason for the banks and financial institutions not to welcome the lower rates, unless they are content to practice usury. Continuing to charge 20 percent interest on loaned money when the prime rate is no more than 4.5 percent is not fair to the borrower, nor is it equitable in any sense of the word.

Why, then, are the banks so sensitive, so negative, about the recently proposed change in credit card rates? This question was answered by S. A. Ravid, Professor of Finance at Columbia University, in the *New York Times*.

> The average consumer charges about $2000 a month. Seven of the ten largest credit card issuers charge a rate of 19.8%, which compounds to 21.7% a year, not the stated 19.8% they advertise. If consumers pay the entire balance each month, they accrue no finance charges. However, if they fail to pay $200.00, they should be charged 1.65% on that $200 the following month, a charge of $3.30. Instead, depending on the rate at which subsequent charges accrue, the charge may be as much as 1.65% on $2,200, or $36.30. This is equivalent to a rate of 18.15% a month, or 640% a year. If the customer does not pay only $10.00 of the outstanding balance, the effective rate could reach the stratospheric level of 331% a month.

There are many examples, similar to the ones in this chapter, that demonstrate the destructive practices of greed and creative calculations that have brought both our economy and our ecology to the brink of disaster. The only way to prevent impending economic hardship is through economic-political measures and policies based on prudent, constructive, and equitable approaches and decisions.

13

Taxation and Tax Policy in Environomics

One of the most effective tools for realizing the concepts of environomics is a well-thought-out tax policy, based primarily on tax incentives, tax penalties, and proper taxation methods. Of equal importance is the proper channeling of tax revenues derived from policies and penalties based on environmental goals. It is imperative that these monies be applied to tax incentives and tax credits that will encourage and promote environmentally friendly practices throughout the economic activities. Although a variety of economic-political measures will be needed, the imposition of environmental incentives combined with environmental taxes and tax penalties will be a major factor in the attainment of environmentally safe prosperity.

The philosophy and approach behind a tax policy consistent with the principles of environomics differ in theory, as well as practice, from those of conventional tax and fiscal policies. The main objective of conventional policy is to generate revenues for financing public and private households and other expenditures, as well as keeping the economy afloat. Little or no thought is given to the environmental impact or the long-term economic ramifications. The single goal of the environomics-based taxation policies under discussion here is to accomplish an environmentally safe, general prosperity.

One of the main reasons for the lack of an environmentally protective policy is the fact that the supporters of the market-oriented economic theory believe that the forces and instruments of market-oriented economies alone will be effective in resolving environmental problems and channeling development in the proper direction, but experience has shown us that this is not the case. Some sort of tax policy must be used to help achieve this goal.

The contention of the proponents of market-oriented economy is that the producer and consumer will be led to behave in an environmentally responsible manner by the incentives and burdens created by price signals within that economy. They rely on the common approach that once a product or service becomes rare, the price begins to escalate until a balance is reached between supply and demand or until an attempt is made to provide a substitute. The belief is that in the long run, the balance between supply and demand will be realized, one way or another. However, this is only a theory. Although the theory may be true in many cases, where environmental issues and raw material availability are concerned, the flaws in the theory became apparent.

The self-healing forces of the market-oriented economy totally ignore the fact that the entrepreneur within the system is motivated to maximize profits and minimize expenses, a motivation that precludes implementing measures to protect the economy and our natural resources. Whenever the entrepreneur takes into consideration the environmental effects of resource allocation, production, distribution, and consumption, an additional cost is incurred, which could affect the competitive edge as well as the profit margin for the product. This will not change unless a climate is created that provides consistent restriction and reward.

If an entrepreneur uses environmentally friendly resources and production methods, the price of the product may be higher than that of less–environmentally concerned competitors. If such is the case, the product and the company will not last long in the marketplace, unless the business person is fortunate enough to find a niche market among environmentally conscious customers willing to pay the higher price to promote their principles. In short, a market-oriented economy cannot resolve the environmental problems when environmental considerations would result in lowering or eliminating profits. Producers, as well as consumers, must be encouraged in the desired direction. A better way must be developed to resolve these problems, a way that reaches beyond reliance on the market forces for a remedy.

Taxes could be an effective instrument in achieving this goal. However, as we have said, it must be made clear that tax policies under environomics — taxation in the interest of an environmentally safe general prosperity — differ in concept and approach from those of the conventional taxation and fiscal policy. The single goal of taxation in environomics is to accomplish an environmentally safe general prosperity. Although I am aware that any kind of taxation appears to be unpopular — something a politician would not wish to deal with voluntarily but would prefer to avoid as long as possible — the approach to taxation within environomics lacks many of the negatives of our current policies. Once the concept and its merits are well-understood and correctly implemented, taxation would no longer suffer the current lack of popularity and support.

It is important that we understand that the issues and values involved in any discussion of taxation and environmentally positive policies are of a subjective nature and their importance may differ from one country to another. For this reason, it is very difficult to develop one specific tax policy that would have global application and could be universally implemented. Issues that have priority in one country may be of no significance to another. This is true not only when comparing industrial with Third World countries but also when comparing two industrial nations that have different life-styles.

Existing practices to protect the environment from destructive economic activities include prohibiting the use of certain products or production methods, imposing various restrictions regarding transportation of poisonous materials, levying taxes for the recycling of garbage (such as aluminum cans and newspapers), and setting limits and thresholds for air-polluting toxic emissions. In critical cases, when violations of the law could be detrimental, violators are risking financial punishment and also face the possibility that their plant or operation could be closed down. Tax incentives, as opposed to penalties, have had a greater degree of effectiveness in moving many companies to employ environmentally sustainable operations, thus reducing the harm to the environment and the level of pollution to a tolerable limit. This latter measure has not been used as advantageously as it could be because of lack of funds or the fear of losing tax revenues.

In spite of these and similar measures, the positive impact on protecting the environment has been very limited. One of the primary reasons for this has been the lack of coordination and long-range goals. These measures alone are not sufficient to promote optimal protection of the environment. Further, these measures include gaps in many areas that make implementation ineffective, such as the use of land for garbage and waste landfills and the use and abuse of energy sources. It is imperative that a series of measures be implemented to lead to the realization of set economic and environmental goals. The combination of different tax measures and policy would help in achieving this.

From the viewpoint of environomics, implementation of an environmentally based tax policy should aim at achieving the five objectives listed below.

1. It should help to protect the environment by phasing out ecologically detrimental production methods and products and

replacing them with environmentally safe production methods and products.

2. It should encourage the increased use of prosperity-inducing technologies (PITs) and other principles of environomics while simultaneously contributing to the phasing out of prosperity-decreasing technologies (PDTs).

3. It should help to protect and extend our fossil energy resources and other raw materials by employing, promoting, and improving high-efficiency technologies and methods of conservation and recycling, as well as other environmentally sound approaches.

4. Efforts must be made to ensure that the employed measures do not strangle the economy. The implementation of proper and positive tax policies should have, at the least, a neutral effect on economic conditions.

5. Realization of the first four objectives, along with improved and more equitable conventional fiscal policies, should lead to creation of general prosperity in real terms.

Implementation of this series of goals is essential if the environment and the economy are to be made compatible and a general prosperity within a safe environment is to be realized. The description of these goals makes the lack of substance of the existing policy and the implemented punitive measures even more clear. The isolated efforts to impose financial punishment on the violators are too few and too ineffective to restore sanity from an ecological standpoint. In addition, they lack the long-term effects necessary to further develop the required environmental goals and channel the economic activities in a direction that would be both economically and environmentally sound and applicable.

Before any nation can effectively implement a tax policy based on environomics, that country must clearly identify the long-term goals it intends to achieve. A number of questions must be addressed: Where does the country want to be in a decade or two regarding its environment and economy? How much pollution is it willing to accept and tolerate and under what circumstances? What kinds of plants and animals are going to be protected? Which ones should be allowed to die out? What level of quality is required in drinking water and food? What standard of living is desired in the future, and what are the definitions and priorities surrounding that standard of living (for example, will we maintain the goal of two-car families or will we move toward an efficient and convenient mass transit system)? What level of health care is to be provided to all people?

If the society progresses to a primarily leisure society, how are people going to be entertained, enlightened, challenged, and stimulated?

In reality, we must find short- and long-term answers not only to environmental and economic questions but also to social and political questions. Once these and similar questions are satisfactorily answered and it has become the political goal of a nation to realize the subsequently defined goals, implementation of efforts to achieve these goals could be started through a rigorously followed tax policy. The objectives of a tax policy based on the concepts and philosophies of environomics can assure realization of the goals, and this will result in a general prosperity and safe environment.

A tax policy based on environomics would be composed of three basic instruments: taxation of undesired products; tax penalties for violations of environmental safety and protection in any phase of resource allocation, production, distribution, or consumption; and tax incentives for environmentally conscious enterprises. Although the implementation of taxation and tax penalties would directly generate revenues, the latter could also generate indirect revenues. There is little doubt that the conversion, through tax incentives, of an environmentally obsolete industry into a modern and environmentally friendly production facility could create a new and vigorous source of revenues through employment and sales. This is particularly important if the facility would have gone out of business had it not been converted. A temporary tax credit or some other type of tax incentive is probably the least expensive method of implementing the conversion of an environmentally obsolete facility to a modern and environmentally friendly production facility, and this could become a healthy source of ongoing revenue.

All companies are mortal, and if nothing is done to rejuvenate an obsolete structure, a company may well die. Many once-familiar companies — Eastern Airlines, Pan Am, RCA — have disappeared from the marketplace for reasons that go beyond labor/management disputes. Does not their mortality prove that an obsolete structure leads to the death of a company, whether this is brought about by an obsolete social structure, obsolete production facilities, or a lack of innovation? On the other hand, Chrysler Corporation was saved by restructuring and modernization, actions that prevented the company from becoming nothing but a part of our corporate history.

Any country that wants to be prepared and equipped for the environmental demands of the twenty-first century must begin now to move seriously in that direction. At the same time, we must recognize that corporations, headed by chief executive officers who are determined to maximize profits, will not voluntarily commit to the additional expenditures for restructuring, especially at the cost of dwindling profits and loss of executive positions. A viable tax policy must be developed to help ease this process in the interest of the future economy and environment of the country. Corporations that are driven by the "bottom line" expectations of shareholders will need the double-edged policy of penalties and incentives to justify the necessary expenditures for conversion to an environmentally friendly facility or service.

The realization of the objectives of environomics, through the implementation of such a tax policy, may require a single measure in some areas and a combination of approaches in other fields. Once the merits and diverse potential of these instruments are clearly understood, there should be little fear of the repercussions. In some instances, the decision may be to phase out PDTs and environmentally obsolete production methods and goods while increasing the efficiency of technologies in other areas for the sake of energy conservation. In these cases, tax penalties and tax liabilities could be implemented. At the same time, revenues derived from this source must be used to promote the PITs and the conversion to modern and environmentally sustainable production facilities and products through tax credit incentives.

In imposing tax penalties, the priority should be the threat of taxation liability and tax penalties if the violators do not correct their product or facility within a stipulated period of time (much as was described in promoting alternate energy sources that are environmentally friendly). Only if this initial step does not attain the desired results should the tax penalty be imposed. This allows time for companies and individuals to explore and implement both environmentally safe solutions and the potential for tax incentives to assist in the conversion while providing the general population an opportunity to investigate the potential for employment in the newly created or converted production and service fields and a period of time to adjust to the new consumer products and services that will result.

Because the costs of products made of recycled materials are often higher than those of products based on nonrecycled (new) raw materials, taxation of the latter is required to bring the prices to an even level. The revenues derived from this tax could be used to subsidize the products made from recycled materials, thus lowering their cost somewhat. The end result is that the goods made from nonrecycled materials become more expensive and the recycled goods become less expensive. The current price discrepancy between recycled and "new" paper is a good example of the present incentive to use new raw materials. This approach to creating an equitable price structure as a purchasing incentive must be used judiciously to avoid strangling the economy by simply making everything more expensive in order to reach an average price for a product or service.

One of the key issues involved in the use of taxation within environomics is that revenues received from environmental taxes and tax penalties must be reserved exclusively for improvements and incentives in the environmental area. If a tax is levied on gasoline, those revenues cannot be used to reduce or eliminate taxes in another area, nor can they be used to support an unrelated program. There is no intent to create a new source of tax revenues that will replace an existing revenue source. Monies from environmental tax penalties and tax liabilities are meant to be applied to the area that created the revenue. These monies should be used for the modernization of production plants through tax incentives and subsidies or to create substitutes for gasoline or to enforce the use of smaller and more efficient vehicles . . . in other words, environmental tax revenues must be applied to the goal of creating environmentally friendly solutions. If this money is not dedicated to the promotion of environmentally friendly facilities and production methods, the tax penalties have not created a real solution, only an additional financial burden on the general population.

Another reason this tax revenue must not be used to replace any current revenues is the fact that sooner or later, this source of revenue will be greatly reduced and eventually eliminated as more and more companies and individuals institute policies and procedures that decrease or eliminate the need for environmental taxes or tax penalties. As the taxation policy accomplishes its objectives and draws closer to the goals of environomics, the revenues from this source become less and less. If other tax sources have been eliminated, we would face a tax revenue deficit, a gap in tax revenue for the country. Politicians would find it difficult to increase taxes, impose a new tax, or reintroduce an old tax.

Do we need to change our entire tax system in order to implement a tax policy that will protect and promote the environment? Although there is little question that tax reform is needed in the interest of creating a more fair tax system for all, there is no need for conflict between the existing tax system and the environmentally based tax policy. Two things are clear: First, we are at the very beginning stage of thinking about an environmental tax policy that will promote the good of both the environment and the economy. Second, serious attention must be paid and more research must be done in this regard.

As mentioned at the beginning of this chapter, any tax policy must take into consideration various countries, economies, cultures, and life-styles.

What works for one country may have little or no value for another. What is a serious environmental concern in one country may be of little or no importance in another nation. As an example, in most of the Western European countries, the use of one-way or disposable bottles has never been an environmentally sensitive issue. Most bottles filled with soft drinks require a deposit upon purchase, which ensures that the consumer will return the bottle to receive the refund. This fact has effectively deterred the use of disposable bottles. Although this has been a successful strategy in those countries, it may not yield the same results in the United States because of the different style of living in this country. However, if we in the United States persist in the use of disposable bottles, we must find a way to deal with the environmental problems caused by their disposal. We have made a start with the practice of recycling these bottles rather than dumping them in landfills and polluting the land for almost a generation or more. However, this solution is still inferior to the methods of the West Europeans. The recycling method of deposit and return is much more environmentally friendly and uses less energy and fewer raw materials. Also, although imposing a deposit on bottles may make a significant difference in some countries, it would be almost meaningless for developing countries, where the majority of the population cannot even get clean water to drink, much less buy any type of beverage.

Clearly, the task involved in creating an effective universal tax policy is a challenging one. The goals in outlining and administering a tax policy not only must take into consideration alternative solutions in every individual case but also must promote the best solution for all involved. The examples above demonstrate the diversity and nature of the problems involved, and more importantly, they highlight the fact that there are a series of diversified problems in different areas plaguing the environment and economy. These require appropriate handling of each individual country's unique and specific problems. Each measure should correspond to the needs, the mentality, and the customs of the particular country involved in order to achieve effective and optimal results. Copying a proven measure from one country to another may not always lead to the same positive outcome.

Because of the scope of this work, it is not my intention to provide detailed answers to individual or specific questions in this chapter. There is no easy answer to questions such as those addressing the optimal way of handling and designating tax amounts for each and every product in order to deter or stimulate its use. There is no single answer to adjusting diverse production methods that vary from country to country.

The purpose of this chapter is to explore the potential of instituting a tax policy based on environomics, as contrasted to our current approach in handling environmental problems through taxation. At present, very little, if any, real attempt has been made to implement a tax policy that will resolve the environmental problems and channel economic activities in the proper direction, one determined by long-term goals and objectives. At best, some isolated action has been taken to prevent damages from running completely out of control.

14

Revitalizing the Economy and Maintaining the Competitive Edge

Many years ago, a Third World nation in Latin America applied to the World Bank for a loan to improve its economy. The World Bank made many conditions for extending the loan, including one that stated that the negative economic conditions in that country — inflation, unemployment, and deficits — should be improved before the money was released. To help this nation fulfill this condition, the World Bank provided experienced economists as advisors to the country's government.

After a few months of intensive study, the group of economists prepared their recommendations for the economic minister of the country. The study revealed that the country suffered enormously from runaway inflation, high unemployment, and chronic deficits. The economic minister countered that he had known of these problems all along. The country had suffered from the conditions for decades and did not need outside experts to come in and tell them what their problems were. What the country needed was someone to tell them how to deal with the problems and eliminate them.

This anecdote demonstrates the situation with the U.S. economy and industry. This book is intended not to simply catalog the problems of which we are all aware, but to attempt to provide rigorous solutions for the problems that exist.

The major obstacle to the revitalization of the U.S. economy and industry and the primary handicap to maintaining the competitive edge is the earlier-discussed problem of short-term thinking on the part of politicians and corporate management. Decisions are linked to immediate payoffs, seeking short-term gains rather than long-term rewards (as is done in Japan). The U.S. approach does not create a culture that thinks about market requirements 20 years in the future.

The Americans have done a great job with military products. Had the same methods been applied to other industries and to the economy in general, the United States would have remained an unbeatable nation in the world. The military-industrial complex in the United States can be focused on the future because the Pentagon pays them to be so while rewarding them profitably for short-term accomplishments. In this instance, there is both short-term and long-term profit motivation. Weapon technology in the United States, with few exceptions, is far more advanced than the combined technologies of the rest of the world. This is a result of the massive efforts expended by the military-industrial complex. The involved industries have plans and blueprints for the next generation of weapon systems, if not for the next two or three generations. Unfortunately, this approach has not been implemented by other industries, perhaps because no government agency is interested in financing such ventures.

The supremacy of nations in the future will be reflected through their economic and industrial strength, now that the Cold War appears to be over. No country can continue to achieve this supremacy through the conventional methods of production nor the current theories of economics if environmental concerns and the depletion of natural resources become strong issues demanding resolution. If these issues become a matter of survival for humanity and the planet, the conventional methods and theories will be obsolete and orientation toward new methods will become imperative. Based on current trends, it is likely that a new orientation will, in fact, become a necessity.

What is the answer? The implementation of the concepts of environomics.

This book has shown the effectiveness of environomics in creating an environmentally safe general prosperity, providing examples and details. Just how would environomics rejuvenate the economy, revitalize industry, and provide for maintenance of our competitive edge?

The implementation of the concept of environomics requires many changes and adjustments, as outlined in this book, if the reconciliation of the environment and the economy is to become a political goal. Even if such a goal never materializes, U.S. industry and economy, along with those of other industrialized nations in the West, need a drastic overhaul to make them competitive both domestically and internationally. This being the case, it is advisable that we take the route leading to the implementation of the concepts of environomics in our economy and industry. This is sound business sense.

Maintenance of the competitive edge would be a natural result as more and more of the concepts are applied. As nations move from the agrarian to industrial, advancing to service and information and finally to leisure, technology, and knowledge, there will be more time for desired activities and less time demanded to meet financial needs. Leisure activities and available hours would provide people the opportunity to study and learn more, develop and improve products, research new ideas and theories. The results of these activities would be integrated into the economy and industry through introduction of new products, services, and other activities, and all participants of the society would benefit. When a nation channels the freed forces from industry and economy into the areas of research and development, it has the natural forces to maintain its competitive edge in the world marketplace.

15

Environomics Implemented:
A Realistic Vision

Picture a future where the concepts of environomics, as presented throughout this work, have been implemented. Look forward in time and see the positive effects of a world where the countries and people enjoy the benefits of a general prosperity and safe environment.

The United States was poised to roll into a new era of economic prosperity and ecological safety at the same time she was in eminent danger of crumbling away.

Many doomsayers had long been predicting the downfall of the United States as a superpower. They saw this as the natural course of events in the destiny of any great world force, regardless of how the decline might take place. The facts, argued the doomsayers, show that after a peak, there must always be a downside. The United States could be no exception. All the great powers of the past had suffered a drastic decline after a period of superiority. Therefore, whether the decline was inflicted by internal or external force, it would occur, considering the historical evidence and the destiny of other great powers in history.

In the case of the United States, the decay of the economy through the accelerating environmental problems made such a prediction even more probable. However, there was one major issue that the doomsayers had not taken into consideration. A series of significant developments were taking place that would shape a bright future for the United States, as well as the rest of the world.

The United States was unlike any other country in the world, unique in one regard. Americans had a strong sense of entrepreneurship and the spirit that went with it. The Japanese and Germans might make a better-quality product than the Americans, but no other country could come close to the new inventions, innovations, discoveries, and developments that routinely occurred there. This very special aspect of the United States was the one factor that the doomsayers discounted or ignored. No other country offered a better environment for developing ideas and the resultant product or service. This climate for new entrepreneurs, encouraging invention and innovation, counterbalanced the awkward behavior of politicians and corporate management.

The political and corporate interests of the United States had long been at odds with the interests of the majority of the population. Meeting the goals and expectations of their supporters, bosses and shareholders had driven the system, and greed frequently overruled the environmental concerns and the overall economic status of the country's less fortunate inhabitants.

As the United States became more excited about and involved with the concept of environomics and the measures to be implemented, various groups of enterprising scientists and engineers in different parts of the country recognized a golden opportunity for marketing their unique inventions and innovations. Not only was big money involved, but also the future possibilities seemed unlimited, similar to the opportunities that had been enjoyed at the beginning of the era of oil, automobiles, and electricity. That era had brought prosperity and comfort. The prosperity, however, had been unbalanced and had been accompanied by devastating pollution and environmental problems. Now, the new era was promising general prosperity combined with a world that had a sound and healthy environment. As in the past, technology was the primary factor that led to U.S. superiority.

Let us step forward in time and consider the possibility of a country following the principles and concepts of environomics.

General Energy Technology, Inc. (GET) rose almost overnight to become one of the nation's most prosperous and well-known firms, specializing in the manufacture of energy-saving technologies. The company had been founded during the oil crisis of the 1970s, but had not gotten off the ground. Development had been stalled by the need for a small electronic component that was the most significant element in a unique, energy-saving device. However, John Newman, a respected and experienced physicist, had joined the company toward the end of the 1980s, and through his efforts and research, the component had been completed and the product was ready for production.

Tom Houston, the founder of the company, recognized that production and marketing of the product would require a major investment and contacted several well-known venture capitalists throughout the country. Sam Davis, one of the most successful supporters of promising entrepreneurs, flew to North Hollywood, California, to meet with Houston at his facility there.

"We received your proposal, and after careful review, it appears to be an interesting and challenging concept. However, we would like more details about your company and your products."

"That's understandable," Houston replied, always eager to discuss his venture. "I formed GET back in 1973 and began manufacturing a tankless water heater, sometimes referred to as the 'instant water heater.' The idea was to make a product that would save energy and water while, at the same time, providing purified water."

"But, what's so unique about this particular unit?"

"The approach and the end result are the key to its difference from others. The idea of an instant water heater is not new, actually dating back to the early 1900s in Europe, where energy has always been costly. Since the 1980s, tankless water heaters have been coming to the United States.

"The conventional instant water heaters employ either coils or cal-rods to heat water. Without exception, they are expensive to operate. The GET instant water heater is the only one that uses plates and explodes the ions in the water. As a result of this approach, not only is the water heated, but it is also purified. In addition, GET's unit is small and compact, fitting in a frame that measures 12 inches by 8 inches by 4 inches. It can be placed anywhere, wherever it's needed."

Davis looked thoughtful. "What does that mean in dollars and cents?"

"It means a tremendous savings. The cost of heating water for a family of six, using a GET unit, would average 20 cents a day or $6 a month, as opposed to the current cost of $60 a month for the use of conventional water tanks. It's a little less than $60 with the other types of instant water heaters."

"That's impressive!"

"Yes, but there's another advantage to the GET unit. Since the system explodes the ions in the water, it also kills all bacteria and eliminates the harmful minerals and chemicals, thus providing healthy, purified water at no additional cost."

Davis glanced at the documents in his lap. "You said your company has been in existence since the mid-1970s, Houston. Why didn't you begin marketing this unit earlier, if it's as great as you have described it?"

"There are a couple of reasons, Mr. Davis. Mainly because of the differing pH values in water from one place to another. Until recently, we lacked the necessary electronic device to adjust the unit to varying conditions and circumstances. Our possibilities for marketing the unit were severely restricted by the fact that we had to practically custom make each one we sold.

"However, since then, Mr. John Newman has joined the company, and he has designed and developed the necessary electronic device to adjust the unit to the different pH values of the water. Now, the unit is practically completed and can be used anywhere, regardless of the difference in pH values. The device is unique, and we hold the patent on it."

"That means, of course, an unlimited market!" Davis commented in appreciation. "And people can recognize measurable energy and water savings, as well as economic advantages, once your unit is available and in use on a large scale?"

"Absolutely. According to our feasibility studies," explained Houston, "each unit could be mass-produced at a tremendous savings, allowing us to market it for $200. The total cost, including installation, would be between $200 and $300, depending on individual circumstances, of course."

"What is the life expectancy of the GET unit?"

"We've designed the unit in such a manner that rarely would there be breakage of any of the functioning parts. In fact, we could practically provide a life-time guarantee for each GET unit, probably a guarantee that would last as long as the original home exists."

"Very interesting. The product seems to meet all the requirements for an economic means of providing a much-needed service to a majority of the population while protecting the environment." Sam Davis peered at Houston over his wire-rimmed glasses. "The unit saves energy and water. It provides hot water for pennies a day. It provides purified water as a natural by-product. On top of that, it's inexpensive to manufacture and the profit margin is excellent. Your guarantee of performance is almost unbeatable. This is one of those rare products that meets environomics' criteria for prosperity-inducing technology."

Sensing that the venture capitalist was leaning toward investment in GET, Tom Houston laid his final arguments carefully before Davis. "Imagine how much water can be saved by simply eliminating the standby losses required by the existing storage tanks. Take that a step farther and imagine the water that would be saved by eliminating the wasted time between when faucets are turned on and when hot water reaches the outlet. On the average, each person wastes three gallons of water every day, just through this waiting period. Multiply that amount by the number of people in each city, each state — throughout the nation — and you can see that the daily savings are substantial. Through the use of this unit, the water shortage can be dealt with in a practical and painless manner, and eventually, the water shortage problem can be eliminated entirely."

Davis pursed his lips, his mind acting like a computerized calculator as he reviewed the numbers and projections necessary for implementing the marketing and production of Houston's unit. "Do you have some idea as to the amount of money required to get this project off the ground on a massive scale?"

"According to the business plan we've developed, we need approximately $3 million. You received some rough estimates in the proposal you have there, but I have a copy of the revised and detailed plan here for your review."

"Let me take it back with me, and I'll be in touch," was Davis' response.

Three weeks later, Sam Davis, Tom Houston, and their attorneys met at the GET offices and signed an agreement that provided GET with the necessary financing to go into full production. The company expanded their operations into a modern plant, the units were approved by the various recognized testing laboratories, and an extensive marketing plan was initiated.

During this period, the major water tank manufacturing companies, realizing the threat, offered a substantial amount of money to buy out the patents from GET, with no success. The intention was to abandon this project altogether. However, GET resisted the attempts from hostile companies. Within a relatively short period, GET began growing in a manner that had been exhibited by only a few rare companies in the history of the industrial revolution and since.

A few months after the investment money from Sam Davis was received and applied, GET's success was dramatically enhanced through the development of a heat exchanger, a further development of the instant water heater technology. The significance of the heat exchanger was obvious from the very first day. The United States still needed large quantities of oil to run its economy and its various industries, regardless of the tremendous amount of savings in the area of water heating. The economy was still vulnerable to a looming external plot constructed around dependency on foreign oil.

During the summer of 1997, the United States reached the height of its critical situation, a circumstance caused by a combination of dependency on imported oil and exposure to threats from the radical nations of the Middle East that could take the United States back to the dark ages of civilization.

The United States had experienced many great and historical moments, many industrial and technological advances that had brought pride to the United States or had acted to preserve its independence, but none could exceed the excitement created on July 19, 1997, when GET's press release appeared across the country. The news not only brought a long-expected feeling of release but also created unlimited hope in the hearts of the U.S. population. Under previous circumstances, the press release would have appeared as a simple item in the business section of the news. However, given the critical issues being faced by the United States as a result of the oil situation, the press release found its way into headlines and received front page coverage in the nation's newspapers, the articles explaining the significance of the news and its anticipated impact on the United States' economic and political independence. Headlines in major papers proclaimed, "California-Based Company Saves America"; "Iranians and Arabs — Keep Your Oil"; "Depletable Oil Reserves of America Reach All Time Height Overnight — Thanks to GET."

What was the magic solution GET had presented to the U.S. public? GET announced the development and availability of the heat exchanger, a unit that generated steam at a very low cost and was small enough to be introduced into existing oil wells. The average individual who did not have an insight into the technical, economic, and geological factors of the oil business did not fully understand what all the excitement was about. The experts, however, were fully able to appreciate the value of the heat exchanger.

Given the available technology, only one-third to one-half of all existing oil reserves worldwide could be reached for exploitation. With this new technology, GET claimed the heat exchanger could easily and inexpensively generate enough steam, and thereby enough pressure, deep inside the oil wells to access at least another one-third of the remaining oil, and it could be done economically. Accompanying the press releases were test results of many so-called dry wells that had pumped oil to the surface for a fraction of previous pumping costs by employing GET's heat exchanger.

As always, the stock market was a swift indicator of the impact this news might have. Immediately following the appearance of the headlines and the press release information, there was a rush on Wall Street and a frenzy of stock purchase. GET's stock began rising rapidly and within hours was trading at $15 a share, an unheard-of amount for a start-up company about which little had been known. As more information became available and more test results were revealed, the stock continued its meteoric climb and, within a matter of weeks, was being traded at $975 a share.

Soon the international oil market and the currency exchange rates began shifting drastically in the United States' favor. Suddenly, the prices of oil and gasoline began a downward spiral, reflecting the level of the early 1990s. At the same time, the U.S. dollar, which had been suffering chronic devaluation, began to regain its original status, returning to its previous dominance in the international market. In a short period of time, the U.S. dollar reached a ratio of one to four with the German mark, the same exchange rate as had been in effect following World War II.

The United States had again become a force to be reckoned with. The change in the international money market reflected two things: the energy conservation policy and the sudden excess in domestic oil. Not only did the United States now have enough oil to satisfy its own needs and become totally independent of foreign oil countries, but it could also export oil to other industrialized nations of the West. This change in status was reflected in the money market, but it also made a tremendous difference in the trade balance, a difference that was certainly advantageous for the United States.

Although GET's contribution to the United States' economic and political independence was critical, another company was quietly developing technology that would be just as crucial and beneficial. Dynamic Power Company (DPC), based in New York state, was another forerunner in leading the United States to its great era of general prosperity. Initially, few people realized the significance of DPC's concept.

During the 1980s and early 1990s, many companies and individuals were working to develop alternate energy sources and technology, recognizing finally that the pollution created by existing energy production methods was extremely harmful to the environment. The conventional wisdom of that time recommended the development of fusion technology and further development of hydrogen as an energy source. The theory was that the energy and fuel derived from these two sources would be plentiful and clean, despite the fact that there was some radioactivity involved in the process. The primary source of the two alternate energy technologies was sea water, a source considered unlimited and cheap. With the exception of some radioactivity released during the fusion process, the technology did not cause any substantial environmental problems. These sources therefore seemed to be the perfect solution to the energy crises.

As this approach gained popularity among the scientific and industrial communities, many companies, such as BMW, began developing a hydrogen-powered car, which carried hydrogen fuel in a high-density, liquefied form to extend its range. General Motors, with an eye to the future, began development of an electric car. Many other car manufacturers followed this trend, seeing it as the future solution. Unfortunately, General Motors and the other companies developing the electric car were only partially right. The major problem, to which none of them attached proper significance, was the fact that these cars would run only on batteries. Because the batteries had to be charged periodically, the full functionality of the cars was limited.

Although fusion technology and hydrogen were definitely a better method for generating energy than the current and conventional methods, the founders of DPC felt they were still not sufficient nor the ultimate solution to the energy crises and the environmental issues. For one thing, fusion and hydrogen technology required centralized power plants, which did not contribute to the independence of the consumers nor to the general prosperity. In addition, the untested technology and the huge financial requirements made these two technologies almost impossible to pursue and sustain.

DPC executives began studying other concepts, searching for one that would fulfill all the criteria of environomics. The product developed by this company soon powered homes, factories, office buildings, cars, boats, and airplanes. It was utilized by highly industrialized countries like the United States, Japan, and Germany and by the less-developed countries such as Ethiopia and Ghana.

DPC's announcement in 1998 created as much excitement as the press releases from GET the previous year. The U.S. public was introduced to the energy amplifier, a unit that would make humanity totally independent of energy problems in the future, regardless of where one lived.

One of the initial press releases stated, "Dynamic Power's Energy Amplifier, a unit about 4 inches square and 12 inches long, with no moving parts, will provide all the electric energy needed to service a four-bedroom house in the frigid zones of Maine or on the hot sands of New Mexico."

A second release promised, "Dynamic Power's Energy Amplifier takes its energy directly from the myriads of infinitely small charged particles that fill the vacuum that surrounds us — our Universe. Thus we have access to a free and inexhaustible source of supply — enough to meet all of our future energy needs."

One of the articles went on to explain the unit more fully. Using a combination of scaler electromagnetic and gravitational waves, DPC had been able to perfect the energy amplifier. The unit used a small, nine-volt, transistor-radio type of battery with a power input of one milliwatt. Out of that was produced 1000 watts of electricity, an amplification of 1 million times. This was more than enough to operate light bulbs, motors, fans, and appliances. Because the unit operated in a steady state, with no moving parts, the device produced an energy gain and could be appropriately termed an "energy amplifier." The unit acted as a gate or switching device for polarized vacuum energy and derived its energy from the nucleus of the atom itself, rather than from the free electrons traveling around the nucleus. Because of the technology, there was no radioactivity involved.

The product developed by DPC did, in fact, meet all the criteria of environomics. It was diversified, it was decentralized, and it cost nothing to operate. Most important was the fact that it created no pollution or radiation. Once you owned the unit, there was no further expense involved. DPC's invention was an ideal model for the decentralized power plant that would truly contribute to the general prosperity in real terms while causing no adverse effect on the ecology of the world.

Another major task remained at the end of the 1990s. The nation had to face the effects of the pollution previously inflicted on the environment. As more and better technologies were developed, based on the concepts of environomics, many of the previous environmental problems were avoided. However, existing problems needed to be dealt with.

One of the major concerns was the threat of the oil-based hazards that had already polluted lakes, rivers, oceans, and surrounding grounds. The pollution of the ground by the oil-based hazards was critical, as it continued to penetrate deeper and deeper into the ground water reservoir. Eco-Pro, Inc., a Tampa-based firm whose name was derived from the words "ecology" and "protection," was one of the pioneer companies to foster a concept to clean up oil-based environmental hazards. Eco-Pro developed a kind of emulsifier that, once applied to any kind of oil-based pollution, transformed the pollutant into a gel. When the gel dried, it became a harmless, sand-like powder. Availability of the emulsifier made it possible to resolve the pollution problems in all areas, from underground soil to the beaches and shorelines.

Eco-Pro, Inc. became a multinational corporation within a few years of developing this unique product and maintained its position by improving existing emulsifiers and continually developing new ones. A significant development was an emulsifier that transformed asbestos into a harmless sand, solving one of the major problems of the interior environment effectively and inexpensively. Another of the products resolved the problem of fertilizers that had been used in agriculture and were beginning to contaminate the ground water; this particular emulsifier was injected into the ground, where it spread to trace the fertilizers and dissolve them into harmless sand.

Through the continued application of Eco-Pro's various emulsifiers, the planet earth once again was clean and its natural beauty was restored. Even though there were periodic oil spills, reminiscent of the Valdez, Alaska disaster in the 1980s, the spills were not nearly as destructive, because the emulsifiers counteracted the effects of such accidents. Although much progress had been made, work remained to be done.

Having become a successful champion in the ecological industry, Eco-Pro began examining the problems of nuclear waste. The firm received a grant from the United States Department of Energy in the year 2000, and encouraged by subsequent tax incentives, the firm developed a technology to decontaminate existing nuclear waste through the neutralization of its radioactivity. As a result, Eco-Pro recognized enormous financial benefits from both local and foreign governments who had to deal with radioactive nuclear waste.

As a follow-on to the valuable experience the company gained in decontaminating nuclear waste and neutralizing radioactivity, Eco-Pro got involved in developing methods and technology to deactivate and dismantle existing nuclear power plants in the United States and around the world. As a result of DPC's energy amplifiers, nuclear power plants had outlived their usefulness. The amplifiers were being used as the dominant source of energy in the United States and worldwide. The population recognized that the nuclear power plants posed a serious threat, sitting like time bombs waiting to explode.

Meantime, the protection of wildlife and natural beauties and resources was being achieved through a series of legislative mandates at both the national and state levels, assuring that the natural balance of the environment would be achieved and then maintained for future generations.

At the same time that this industrial and environmental revolution was taking place in the United States, drastic changes were occurring in the area of health care. Based on the concept of environomics, new, multi-specialty clinics had begun to appear all over the country, following the lead of a few prototype clinics that had enjoyed impressive medical and financial success.

The innovation was started by a group of business people who were willing to risk a relatively small amount of money to test the venture.

They formed a corporation called General Health, Inc. (GHI), leased three large, abandoned grocery stores in Miami, Florida, and converted them to different types of multispecialty clinics.

The first clinic specialized in alleviating pain of all kinds and employed doctors who practiced in orthopedics, chiropractic medicine, and neurology, as well as experts in physical and sports therapy. The second clinic concentrated on family medicine, obstetrics, gynecology, and pediatrics. The third specialized in internal medicine.

From the first day, the prototype clinics were successful for two reasons: the services were better and the prices lower than in conventional clinics. While the conventional clinics in Miami began to lose patients, the GHI clinics had more than they could handle. Very soon, other clinics of a similar nature began to operate in the Miami area. Soon a franchising plan was developed to implement the concept across the country.

One of the amazing facts of this success story was the relatively small investment that had been required. From a $15 million investment in three prototype clinics, GHI created a multi-billion dollar company. Much of the money was derived from franchising, and eventually, GHI enjoyed a strong presence in almost every country in the world.

Seeing the success of the project, many doctors joined the clinics as employees. Others, with enterprising talents and their own financial resources, began to copy the concept of GHI, forming corporations to operate clinics of the same nature. They recognized the threat the new clinics posed and determined that the best defense was to take advantage of the new trend. Soon, there were a number of different corporations offering clinical services similar to those developed by GHI, each trying to offer better services and remain as competitive as possible.

The result was much the same as the growth of the fast food industry following the astonishing success of McDonald's. GHI remained the leader in the health care industry, partly due to the international franchising of their clinics. The people of the United States finally had available universal health care that was competent and affordable and that served as a model for other countries of the world.

By the year 2010, the four companies discussed here headed the list of Fortune Five Hundred companies in the United States. GHI held first place, followed by DPC and Eco-Pro, with GET in fourth place.

GET had run into a critical period when the products developed by DPC hit the market and people became less concerned about saving energy. The company had to reorient to the new attitude or go out of business. Reviewing the market and future projections, GET made the decision to get involved in the manufacture of high-quality cars, automobiles based on the concept of environomics. The vehicles were of modular design and powered by DPC's self-perpetuating magnetic motors, a system based on the energy amplifier technology. The timely transition to automobile manufacturing saved the company and provided financial stability and a profit figure that allowed GET to retain its position near the top of the Fortune Five Hundred listing.

All four of these companies took advantage of the needs of the world and the people, providing solutions that were based on the concept of environomics. There had been a desperate need for universal and afford-able health care; alternate energy sources were required if the United States was to maintain its position in the world and not be dependent upon the whims of the Middle East leaders; the environmental problems had become so severe that the U.S. public, as well as other people throughout the world, were demanding that government address the issue in some positive manner.

Today, this is only a dream, an illusion, a vision. However, the vision is not that far from becoming reality, if only the people of this nation demand it, the politicians provide the necessary decisions and incentives, and the industry leaders engage in sincere efforts to accomplish the task.

16

Conclusion

The final questions to be answered revolve around the potential implications involved in the realization of the concept of environomics and whether it could actually resolve the economic and ecological ills of the world.

The first requirement is that environomics be clearly understood — its concept, its validity, its effectiveness, and its unquestionable advantage over other, more conventional, concepts and ways of thinking. It is necessary to realize that environomics and its concepts are the ultimate answer to creating an environmentally safe prosperity. Until a general prosperity, or at the least the potential for such, is created for all people and nations, poverty and the struggle for survival and independence will continue to be a threat to the existence of the planet and its inhabitants. Under these conditions, a new order cannot be established and expected to flourish.

What are the implications from a political standpoint? Can there be any doubt that a candidate who made environomics the agenda of a political race would not enjoy great popularity during the campaign and garner the necessary votes to be elected to office? What citizen would vote against a candidate who intends to lead the nation toward a general prosperity while curing the ecological problems at the same time? Who would be against a politician who promises to cure the economic, environmental, and social ills that are threatening everyone?

What about corporate management, industry leaders, and capitalists? Their major task will be to adjust their way of thinking, seeing numbers and dimensions in real, not nominal, terms. They will have to get away from the illusions that create numbers that do not reflect real values. Once this is done, the rest is easy.

They could still strive toward high profits and healthy bank accounts. They could still maintain their percentage of wealth compared with others. The ratio is no different when comparing $100 with $10 than it is when comparing $1,000 with $100; in both cases, the richer individual has 90 percent more money than the poorer.

There is one critical difference. In an economy based on the concept of environomics, the numbers would not be inflated; they would be real. There is little reason that a capitalist would suffer any reduction in capital or profit or lose control of the business. In real terms, the ratios would remain the same.

How can one be sure that the concept of environomics will work and fulfill its promises, in spite of all the sound economic and ecological reasons presented in this work? Consider the following:

Had the world economy grown qualitatively, along the quantitative growth of 2 percent to 4 percent annually common among the industrialized nations of the West in the years following World War II, we would have an inventory large enough to satisfy everybody's need for material goods. On the other hand, the environmental damages would have been considerably reduced. Add to that fact the features of the concept of environomics, and the situation is even more improved. If utopia is ever to be realized, it can be done by applying the concept of environomics.

The final questions remain. How do we implement the concept of environomics politically and how could a politician win an election by making environomics the primary platform plank? Before attempting to answer this question, we need to take a close look at the present circumstances of politicians and political power centers.

It is commonly accepted that most politicians have become quite adept at looking out for their own interests and self-enrichment. The special-interest groups assure that politicians will either promote legislation beneficial to that group or will block any attempts at legislation that might threaten or jeopardize their concerns by the simple expedient of gifts to other legislators or promises of future cooperation on other issues. Most incumbents are career politicians, well aware that there is little to threaten their position, barring involvement in some major scandal made known to the population through the efforts of the media.

Recently, the awareness of the people has been rising, and there are many who question how the government has managed to gobble up nearly 40 percent of the gross national profit while not providing the services for which taxes have been paid. The people of the United States are becoming aware of the waste and mismanagement that seem to be epidemic within government.

The two-party system does not seem to be accomplishing its purpose. The Democrats want to tax the wealthy to finance their economic and political goals, while the Republicans attempt to reach these same goals with borrowed money. The Democratic policies create a lack of incentive among the population, and the Republicans seem determined to postpone the burdens of finance, leaving the problem to the next generation. The disillusionment of the people — the voters — has begun to rise, and their dissatisfaction with the political system and politicians is apparent.

In 1990, voters in three states — California, Colorado, and Oklahoma — passed a proposition setting as limit of three terms, or six years, for state assembly members and two terms, or eight years, for state senators. All other statewide elected officials are limited to a maximum of eight years.

That same year, the Big Green initiative on California's ballot lost by a margin of one to two. Although the purpose of the Big Green initiative was a positive intention to implement measures to protect the environment, the proposed solutions would have been costly. The U.S. public, not yet convinced of the necessity of the measures and facing an uncertain economy, were unwilling to encourage the initiative. Similar Green measures lost in five other states, dismaying ecology-minded citizens and groups.

Politicians and environmentalists are going to be confronted more and more often with this situation in the years to come, as political offices are up for grabs and environmental legislation is proposed. The standards for politicians are being set higher and higher. Environmentalists can be successful in realizing their goals only by making sure that their proposals and concepts do not have an adverse effect on the standard of living of the population, placing an additional financial burden on individuals who cannot afford it.

Voters are disillusioned with the present politicians and the current political establishment as a result of their inability to satisfy the economic needs of the people and the environmental needs of the planet. Any politician, whether at the state or the national level, would have an excellent chance to attract voters by making prosperity for the people and protection for the environment the two central campaign topics.

It may well be that many politicians find these two topics interesting and viable and use them to build their platforms. However, they do not provide answers to the critical issues that surround the questions. Environomics and its concept provide the necessary solutions to the issues of health care, employment, energy, social security, and housing.

Prosperity is the key, particularly when joined with protection of our ecology and environment.

A four-point program would make the implementation of environomics possible from a political standpoint. The first point would be legislation that requires that industrial goods comply with the concept of environomics. Goods featuring the concept would be endorsed and promoted by the use of tax incentives based on guidelines requiring full warranty performance by the manufacturer. (An example of this approach was given during the discussion of solar energy.) Where warranty performance is concerned, the more comprehensive the warranty provided, the higher would be the tax incentive.

The second point would be tax incentives provided to entrepreneurs who were willing to provide health care in accordance with the environomics concept, based on multispecialty clinics. The already-established Medicare and Medicaid patient programs would provide further incentives if the patients were to use these clinics exclusively.

Legislation should be passed that protects wild life, nature, and the remaining natural resources.

Finally, monetary and fiscal policies should be introduced that would make purchasing and owning a home, car, and other necessary, but expensive, items a possibility for all people. A significant contribution toward creating general prosperity would be the reduction of interest rates to a minimum. High interest rates have virtually bankrupted the United States and currently enslave the working middle class for many years longer than necessary to attain a given standard of living. In many cases, interest costs make paying for goods take longer than the goods last while driving up the cost of replacement goods. Many of our economic problems would solve themselves if this trend was reversed.

Sooner or later, almost all of us are going to become old, usually much sooner than we expect and before we are prepared for it. Not the least of the problems associated with aging is a decline in our standard of living. Although the creation of our Social Security system was supposed to prevent this, without independent means, such as wise investments or an extensive savings program, few of us will be able to maintain the standard of living we enjoyed during our working years.

True "social security" implies sufficient wealth to support oneself in the years of retirement. Home ownership is a cornerstone of security. Simply saving 10 or 15 years' worth of mortgage interest would in itself make a person quite secure. The housing industry is the backbone of the economy; the more people who acquire houses, the greater the prosperity of the entire nation. The approach proposed here, temporarily redirecting a portion of an individual's Social Security contribution toward the payment of principal on a home mortgage, would greatly contribute to general prosperity by creating steadily expanding employment and preventing exploitive interest practices.

Some may view these measures critically and raise questions regarding their validity. For instance, if we become too strict with warranty performance requirements, many manufacturers may claim they cannot comply with the regulations, or they may say if they do comply with the new rules and regulations, the cost will put them out of business. This raises some interesting questions. Does that attitude and concern not reflect strong indications that there are currently problems with shoddy or low-quality products? Why should the consumer be penalized for this? The issue of warranty performance is one example of a change in attitude and expectation that can be introduced gradually, reaching its maximum potential over a period of a few years.

Last, but not least, one cannot emphasize enough the need to rigorously follow prudent and constructive economic-political measures. Arbitrary policies, based on the "quick fix" approach, must be totally avoided, as the potential escalation of the social costs and environmental destruction is devastating. The same emphasis must be directed toward rational behavior and the prevention of wastefulness in the economy. In other words, the economic-political goals should be to maintain a high standard of living for individuals who have currently achieved such while creating the possibilities for others to attain this.

"Quick fixes" such as minor tax cuts for the middle class or tax-the-rich schemes are not solutions and are counterproductive. The economy needs more than short-term euphoria. By employing environomic concepts to formulate carefully targeted tax incentives, the government can create immediate new employment and assure lasting general prosperity.

The focus of tax incentives must be prosperity-inducing technologies (PITs). This means targeting industries that employ PITs, such as environmentally friendly alternate energy sources, or the creation of industries that would employ PITs. Incentives should also be used to encourage other industries to adopt environomic, prosperity-enhancing concepts, such as extending the useful life of their products and modular designs that allow integration of future technological improvements. A simple measure of extended product life would be manufacturers' warranties.

These measures would contribute to general prosperity and enhance tax revenues for the government through the creation of new, permanent employment, while reducing the cost burden of unemployment.

The benefits of environomics will be achieved through policy decisions and actions of government and industry, both of which are driven by market forces. Industry is responsive to the demands of its customers, and government responds to the demands of the voters.

To implement environomics will require virtually no investment on the part of government. Government's role is to define goals, formulate the policies, and set the rules necessary to achieve those goals. Government's most efficient means to steer the economy to achieve these goals is through tax incentives, in the form of credits and penalties. Properly applied, these need cost nothing; in fact, the net result will be more tax revenue. In the long run, this can lead first to a balanced budget and, eventually, to a permanent reduction of tax rates for everyone.

Environomic concepts apply not only to the manufacturing sector but also to the service sector. A prime example is the health care industry. Tax incentives can be used to increase productivity and efficiency, to make health care universally available and affordable.

U.S. industry must not wait for the government to initiate such policies. Tax incentives are not a substitute for the profit motive. Environomic concepts offer boundless opportunities for sustainable growth, and industry should embrace them and act upon them for its own sake, as well as for the sake of the nation and the world.

In the 1970s, the U.S. auto industry was not prepared for the changing needs of the market and lost a great deal of the market share to the Japanese and Germans. The needs of the twenty-first century marketplace are clear: products and technologies that are environmentally sustainable. Failure to recognize this now and to act accordingly will result in further export of employment and a decline in prosperity.

It is absurd to blindly promote arbitrary quantitative economic growth with the illusion that this can continue forever. Is it not more rational to provide people the opportunity of maintaining their standard of living while gradually reducing the need for work? Is it not more rational to make the resulting work hours available to other workers, as opposed to paying an exorbitant amount of money to protect jobs?

Consider the cost of protecting various jobs in the U.S. work force. To protect one job in the U.S. steel industry through the use of tariff barriers runs as high as $1 million; in the orange juice industry, the cost is $240,000; in book manufacturing, the cost of trade barriers per job saved is $100,000. These costs are borne by the U.S. consumer, not the corporate officers, politicians, or foreign citizens.

It is high time to be seriously concerned, to ask critical questions, and to seek real answers. Although no one can accurately predict the future, it is important that we at least have a sound vision. The time of following shortsighted politicians and policymakers is over; we can no longer afford their policies, economically or environmentally. The stakes are high for all of us, but especially for our children and their children.

We have a responsibility to ourselves, our neighbors, and our planet to avoid this potential. The concepts of environomics must be implemented.

Environomics is a practical approach to resolving environmental problems while revitalizing and redirecting economic activities to create permanent prosperity. It is applicable to the economic and environmental problems in the United States and throughout the world. Application of environomic concepts will result in the preservation and repair of the environment, while establishing a higher standard of living for everyone who shares this planet. For Americans, environomics represents a new era of world leadership as the United States is transformed from an industrial society to a technological society and, finally, to a prosperous, leisure society.

The task is formidable, but not impossible. The direction is clear. Environomics provides the guidelines. There is no need to sacrifice our environment to achieve prosperity, but we need not forego prosperity to preserve the environment.

Let us work together, for our own sakes and for the sake of generations to come, to create a system that will provide security and prosperity for all while protecting and preserving our environment.

The seeds of a better future are in our hands. It is our responsibility to plant those seeds and nurture them to provide a bountiful harvest for the earth and all of its people.

Appendix: Comparison of Current Economic Policy and Environomics — Their Impacts in Different Sectors

Sector	Current Economics	Environomics
Economic		
Inflation	Stimulating	Dampening
Employment	Unemployment rates high and costly	Permanent full-time employment
Balance of payments	Not balanced	Balanced
Trade balance	Not balanced	Balanced
Economic cycles	Periodic ups and downs	Steady, positive developments
Productivity	Periodic improvements	Steady, positive developments
Economic growth	Nominal	Real
Quantitative economic growth	Limited and arbitrary	Only in area of PITs, until saturation of the market is achieved
Qualitative economic growth	Nonexistent	Realized indefinitely
Interest	Manipulative, used for transfer of wealth	Nonmanipulative, allowed only as compensation to banks for handling money
Interest rates	Medium to high, with exploitive features	Low, with tendency toward zero
Prosperity	Nominal and diminishing	Real and can be increased indefinitely
Quality of life	Limited and diminishing	Can be improved indefinitely
Standard of living	Diminishing	Would improve drastically
Policy		
Domestic	No balance in economic and social systems	Balanced economic and social systems
Foreign	Hostile and exploitive	Constructive and conciliatory
Fiscal	Exploitive	Constructive
Health care	Very costly, cost uncontrollable, availability and quality diminishing	Cost effective, universal availability, high quality

Housing	Exploitive	Constructive and low cost
Social security	Limited and nominal, causing decline in standard of living	Real, no decline in standard of living
Industrial	Insecure future	Secure future
R & D	Diminishing, becoming costly	Stimulating, cost effective
Technology	PDTs are promoted, PITs are neglected	PITs would be promoted and PDTs phased out
Arms race	Exorbitant economic and social cost	Limited cost
Energy	Nonexistent, highly costly with very high social cost	Low-cost policy, no social cost involved
Environmental	Moderately supported, colliding with economic interests	Economic and environmental interests would mutually promote and enhance each other
Social		
Housing	Increased homelessness and lack of ownership, due to exorbitant cost	Increased housing availability and ease of ownership
Justice	Limited and diminishing	Would improve
Safety	Limited and diminishing	Would improve tremendously
Education level	Diminishing and becoming exorbitantly expensive, often unaffordable	Would be stimulated and affordable
Pollutant Levels		
Air	High and dangerous	Balanced and low
Water	High and devastating	Balanced and low
Land	High and devastating	Balanced and low

177

Sector	Current Economics	Environomics
Natural Resources		
Water	Abused and wasted	Protected
Land	Abused and devastated	Protected
Raw materials	Wasted	Protected
Fossil energy	Wasted	Protected

Source: Compiled by author.

Bibliography

Abfall vermeiden. *Leitfaden fuer eine oekologische Abfallwirtschaft.* Frankfurt am Main: Fischer Taschenbuch Verlag, 1989.

Akhtarekhavari, Farid. *Die Oelpreispolitik der OPEC-Laender, Grenzen, Gruende und Hintergruende.* Munich: Weltforum Verlag, 1975.

Akhtarekhavari, Farid. *Die OPEC im weltwirtschaftlichen Spannungsfeld, Ein Beitrag zur Discussion um die "neue Weltwirtschaftsordnung."* Munich: Weltforum Verlag, 1976.

Altner, G., and I. Schmitz-Feuerhake. *239 Pu: Die Gefahren der Plutoniumwirtschaft.* Frankfurt am Main: Fischer Taschenbuch Verlag, 1980.

Anwar, Muhammad. *Modeling Interest Free Economy, A Study in Macro-Economics and Development.* Herndon, Va.: The Internatinal Institute of Islamic Thought, 1987.

Auf dem Wege nach Utopia. Frankfurt am Main: Campus Verlag, 1985.

Aufgabe Zukunft. *Qualitatives Wachstum.* Frankfurt am Main: Europaeische Verlagsanstalt, 1972.

Aufgabe Zukunft. *Qualitaet des Lebens.* Frankfurt am Main: Europaeische Verlagsanstalt, 1972.

Balck, H. and R. Kreibich. *Evolutionaere Wege in die Zukunft, Wie lassen sich komplexe Systeme managen?* Weinheim: Beltz Verlag, 1991.

Bartlett, Bruce. *Supply Side Economics in Action.* Westport, Conn.: Arlington House, 1981.

Bechmann, Arnim. *Umwelt braucht Frieden, Umweltzerstoerung durch Ruestung.* Frankfurt am Main: Fischer Taschenbuch Verlag, 1983.

Bernstein, M. C., and J. B. Bernstein. *Social Security, The System That Works.* New York, N.Y.: Basic Books, 1988.

Binswanger, Frisch, Nutzinger, and others. *Arbeit ohne Umweltzerstoerung, Strategien einer neuen Wirtschaftspolitik, Eine Publikation des Bundes fuer Umwelt and Naturschultz Deutschland (BUND).* Frankfurt am Main: S. Fischer Verlag, 1983.

Blohmke, Maria. *Sozialmedizin.* Stuttgart: Ferdinand Enke Verlag, 1986.

Blomstroem, M. and B. Hettne. *Development Theory in Transition: The Dependency Debate and Beyond: Third World Responses.* London: Zed Books, 1987.

Bombach, Gottfried, "Konsum oder Investition fuer die Zukunft?" in: *Qualitatives Wachstum, Series 7,* Frankfurt am Main, Germany: Europaeische

Verlaganstalt, 1972.

Boskin, Michael J. *Reagan and the Economy, The Successes, Failures & Unfinished Agenda*. San Francisco, Calif.: ICS Press, 1989.

Bossel, Hartmut. *Umweltwissen: Daten, Fakten, Zusammenhaenge*. Berlin: Springer Verlag, 1990.

Brown, Lester R., and others. *State of the World, A Worldwatch Institute Report on Progress towards a Sustainable Society*. New York, N.Y.: W. W. Norton, 1991.

Buechele, H. and L. Wohlgenannt. *Grundeinkommen ohne Arbeit, Auf dem Weg zu einer kommunikation Gesellschaft*. Vienna: Europa Verlag, 1985.

Colombo, U., G. Turani. *Der zweite Planet Bericht der Club of Rome*. Vienna: Europa Verlag, 1986.

Contemporary Aspects of Economic Thinking in Islam, Proceedings of the Third East Coast Regional Conference of the Muslim Students' Association of the United States and Canada, April 1968. Brentwood, Md.: International Graphics Printing Service, 1980.

Creutz, H., D. Suhr, and W. Onken. *Wachstum bis zur Krise?* Berlin: Basis Verlag, 1986.

Deppe, F., and S. Kebir. *Eckpunkte Moderner Kapitalismuskritik*. Hamburg: VSA-Verlag, 1991.

Dustdar, Farzin. *Das Modell des Friedens, Aysweg aus der Krise*. Vienna: Horizonte Verlag, 1985.

ESSO, Oeldorado. Hamburg, ESSO, different years.

Fischer, Joschka. *Der Umbau der Industriegesellschaft*. Frankfurt am Main: Vito von Eichborn, 1989.

Fornallaz, Pierre. *Ganzheitliche Ingenieurausbildung, Eine Antwort auf die Technikkritik unserer Zeit*. Karlsruhe: Mueller, 1982.

Gorz, A. *Und Jetzt Wohin?* Noerdlingen: Rotbuch Verlag, 1991.

Grawe, Joachim. *Neue Techniken der Energie Gewinnung*. Stuttgart: Verlag Bonn Aktuell, 1989.

Gruhl, Herbert. *Glueklich werden sein: Zeugnisse oekologischer Weltsicht aus vier Jahrtausenden*. Frankfurt am Main: Ulstein, 1989.

Guggenberger, Bernd. W*enn uns die Arbeit ausgeht*. Munich: Carl Hauser Verlag, 1988.

Gurley, John G. *Challenges to Capitalism, Marx, Lenin, Stalin and Mao*. Reading, Pa.: Addison Wesley, 1988.

Hammong, A. L., W. D. Metz, and T. H. Maugh. *Energy and the Future*. Washington, D.C.: American Association for the Advancement of Science, 1973.

Handy, Charles. *The Age of Unreason*. Boston, Mass.: Harvard Business School Press, 1989.

Hauff, Volker. *Energie-Wende, Von der Empoerung zur Reform*. Munich: Droemersche Verlagsanstalt, 1986.

Hellman, Hal. *Energy in the World of the Future*. New York, N.Y.: M. Evans, 1973.

Hermanns, P. M., and L. Harnisch. *Gesundheit! Danke, aber wer zahlt? Eine Kostenanalyse der Gesundheit Vorschlaege zur Kostendaempfung*. Hamburg: Rowohlt Taschenbuch Verlag, 1988.

Holzapfel, H., K. Traube, and O. Ulrich. *Autoverkehr 2000, Wege zu einem oekologisch und sozial vertraeglichen Strassenverkehr*. Karlsruhe: Mueller, 1988.

Hottel, H. C., and J. B. Howard. *New Energy Technology, Some Facts and Assessments.* Cambridge, Mass.: MIT Press, 1971.

Illich, Ivan. *Limits to Medicine.* London: Marion Boyars, 1976.

Jones, G. S., and J. A. Marini. *The Imperial Congress Crisis in the Separation of Powers.* New York, N.Y.: Pharos Books, 1988.

Kapp, K. William. *Fuer eine oekosoziale Oekonomie.* Frankfurt am Main: Fischer Taschenbuch Verlag, 1987.

Keynes, John Maynard. *The General Theory of Employment, Interest, and Money.* New York, N.Y.: Harcourt, Brace, 1936.

Khavari, Farid. *Vultures: Doctors, Lawyers, Hospitals and Insurance Companies, What's Wrong, and What to Do About It?* Malibu, Calif.: Roundtable Publishing, 1990.

Khavari, Farid. *Oil & Islam, The Ticking Bomb.* Malibu, Calif.: Roundtable Publishing, 1990.

Kieffer, K. W., W. Duerrschmidt, I. Luenzer, and G. Moeller. *Oekologisch denken und handeln, Strategien mittlere Technologie.* Karlsruhe: Mueller, 1988.

Kiplinger, A. H. and K. A. Kiplinger. *America in the Global '90s.* Washington, D.C.: Kiplinger, 1989.

Koch, T. C., J. Seeberger, and H. Petrik. *Oekologische Muellverwendung, Handbuch fuer optimale Abfallkonzepte.* Karlsruhe: Mueller, 1986.

Koesters, Paul Heinz. *Oekonomen veraendern die Weltwirtschafts Theorien, die unser Leben bestimmen.* Hamburg: Goldman Verlag, 1989.

Kortenkamp, A., B. Grahl, and L. H. Grimme. *Die Grenzlosigkeit der Grenzwerte.* Karlsruhe: Mueller, 1988.

Kraemer, Walter. *Die Krankheit des Gesundheitswesen, Die Fortschrittsfalle der modernen Medizin.* Frankfurt am Main: S. Fischer Verlag, 1989.

Krugman, Paul. *The Age of Diminished Expectations, U.S. Economic Policy in the 1990s.* Cambridge, Mass.: MIT Press, 1990.

LaBastille, Anne. *Mama Poc, An Ecologist's Account of the Extinction of a Species.* New York, N.Y.: W. W. Norton, 1990.

Lafontaine, Oskar. *Die Gesellschaft der Zukunft.* Munich: Wilhelm Heyne Verlag, 1989.

Lamm, R. D., R. A. Caldwell, and I. H. Mehlman. *Hard Choices.* Denver, Colo.: The Center for Public Policy and Contemporary Issues, University of Denver, 1989.

Leipert, Christian. *Die heimlichen Kosten des Fortschritts, Wie Umweltzerstoerung das Wirtschaftswachstum foerdert.* Frankfurt am Main: S. Fischer Verlag, 1989.

Lekachman, Robert. *Greed is Not Enough: Reaganomics.* New York, N.Y.: Pantheon Books, 1982.

Lewis, H. W. *Technological Risk.* New York, N.Y.: W. W. Norton, 1990.

Leyendecker, H., and R. Rickelmann. *Exporteure des Todes, Deutscher Ruestungsskandal in Nahost.* Goettingen: Steidl Verlag, 1990.

Lovins, A. B., L. H. Lovins, F. Krause, and W. Bach. *Wirtschaftlicher Energieeinsatz: Loesung des CO_2 Problems.* Karlsruhe: Mueller, 1983.

Lowry, Ritchie P. *Good Money, A Guide to Profitable Social Investing in the '90s.* New York, N.Y.: W. W. Norton, 1991.

Malunat, Bernd M. *Weltnatur and Staatenwelt, Gefahren unter dem Gesetz der Oekologie.* Zurich: Edition Interfrom, 1988.

Matthoefer, Hans. *Interviews und Gespraeche zur Kernenergie.* Karlsruhe: C. F. Mueller, 1976.

Mayer, Helge. *Qualititves Wachstum-Einfuehrung in Konzeptionen der Lebensqualitaet.* Frankfurt am Main: Campus Verlag, 1984.

Meadows, Dennis, et al. *The Limits to Growth.* New York, N.Y.: Universe Books, 1972.

Medvedev, Zhores A. *The Legacy of Chernobyl.* New York, N.Y.: W. W. Norton, 1990.

Mineraloelwirtschaftsverband, Mineraloelzahlen. Hamburg: ACO Druck GmbH, different years.

Monetary and Fiscal Economies of Islam, An Outline of Some Major Subjects for Research. Leichester: Lowe & Carr, 1980.

Nichols, John. *The Sky's the Limit, A Defense of the Earth.* New York, N.Y.: W. W. Norton, 1990.

Neinhaus, Volker. *Islam und moderne Wirtschaft: Positionen, Probleme und Perspektiven.* Graz: Verlag Styria, 1982.

Opielka, Michael. *Die oekologische Frage: Entwuerfe Zum Sozialstaat.* Frankfurt am Main: Fischer Taschenbuch Verlag, 1985.

Perlin, John. *A Forest Journey, The Role of Wood in the Development of Civilization.* New York, N.Y.: W. W. Norton, 1989.

Pestel, Eduard. *Jenseits der Grenzen des Wachstums, Bericht an den Club of Rome.* Stuttgart: Deutsche Verlags Anstalt, 1988.

Redefining Wealth and Progress: New Ways to Measure Economic, Social and Environmental Change, The Caracas Report On Alternative Development Indicators. Indianapolis, Ind.: Knowledge Systems, 1989.

Rossi, Peter H. *Down and Out in America, The Origins of Homelessness.* Chicago, Ill.: University of Chicago Press, 1989.

Ruehl, Walter. *Energiefaktor Erdoels: In 250 Millionen Jahren enstanden, nach 250 Jahren verbraucht?* Zurich: Edition Interfrom, 1989.

Scheer, Hermann. *Die Gespeicherte Sonne, Wasserstoff als Loesung des Energie und Umweltprobleme.* Munich: R. Piper GmbH, 1987.

Sik, O., R. Hoeltschi, and C. Rockstroh. *Wachstum und Krisen: Zur Thoerie und Empirie von Konjunkturzyklen und Wachstumswellen.* Berlin: Springer Verlag, 1988.

Simonis, U. E. *Oekonomie und Oekologie, Auswege aus einem Konflikt.* Karlsruhe: Mueller, 1988.

Simonis, U. E. *Mehr Technik, Weniger Arbeit: Plaedoyers fuer sozial und umweltvertraegliche Technologien.* Karlsruhe: Mueller, 1984.

Sklar, Holly. *Trilateralism, The Trilateral Commission and Elite Planning for World Management.* Boston, Mass.: South End Press, 1980.

Skolimowski, Henryk. *Oeko-Philosophie, Entwurf fuer neue Lebensstrategien.* Karlsruhe: Mueller, 1988.

Spitzley, Helmut. *Die andere Energie-Zukunft, Sanfte Energienutzung statt Atomwirtschaft und Klimakatastrophe.* Stuttgart: Verlag Bonn Aktuell GmbH, 1989.

Streich, Juergen. *Global 1990, Zwischenbilanz der Umweltstudie Global 2000.* Hamburg: Rasch u. Roehring, 1989.

Timm, Herman. *Wie gruen darf die Zukunft sein? Naturbewusstein in der Umweltkrise.* Guetersloh: Guetersloher Verlagshaus Mohn, 1987.

von Thaden, Hans Werner. *Umweltschutz, Umweltpolitik, Gesetzliche Grundlagen praktische Durchsetzung.* Heidelberg: R. v. Decker & C. F. Mueller, 1987.

Umweltbilanz: Die oekologische Lage der Bundesrepublik, Bund fuer Umwelt und Naturschutz Deutschland (BUND). Hamburg: Rasche u. Roehring, 1988.

Viehues, Herbert. *Lehrbuch Sozial Medizin.* Stuttgart: Verlag W. Kohlhammer GmbH, 1981.

Wanniski, Jude. *The Way the World Works.* Morristown, N.J.: Polyconomics, 1978, 1983, 1989.

Weber, Rudolf. *Strom aus tausend Quellen.* Oberboezberg: Olynthus Verlag, 1986.

Weber, Rudolf. *Der sauberste Brennstoff: Der Weg zur Wasserstoff Wirtschaft.* Oberboezberg: Olynthus Verlag, 1988.

Wilhelm, Sighard. *Oekosteuern, Marktwirtschaft and Umweltschutz.* Munich: Beck, 1987.

Wilson, John Oliver. *The Power Economy: Building an Economy That Works.* Boston, Mass.: Little, Brown, 1985.

Woehlcke, Manfried. *Umweltzerstoerung in der Dritten Welt.* Munich: Beck, 1987.

ADDITIONAL SOURCES

Business Week, New York, N.Y.
The Environmental Magazine, Syracuse, N.Y.
Foreign Affairs, New York, N.Y.
Fortune, New York, N.Y.
The Futurist, Bethesda, Md.
Garbage, New York, N.Y.
Health Watch, Louisville, Ky.
Insight on the News, Washington, D.C.
Miami Herald, Miami, Fla.
Newsweek, New York, N.Y.
New York Times, New York, N.Y.
Nuclear Times, Boston, Mass.
OMNI, New York, N.Y.
Rehabilitation Today, Framingham, Mass.
Technology Review, Cambridge, Mass.
Times, New York, N.Y.
U.S. News & World Report, Washington, D.C.
Washington Post, Washington, D.C.
World and I, Washington, D.C.
World Monitor, Boston, Mass.

Index

ABOUT THE AUTHOR

Farid A. Khavari is Chairman of Environomic Research Institute, Inc. in Miami, Florida. He holds an M.A. from the University of Hamburg and a Ph.D. from the University of Bremen.